1300 Missing Missouri Marriage Records

From Newspapers, 1812-1853

by
Lois Stanley
George F. Wilson
Maryhelen Wilson

Southern Historical Press, Inc.
Greenville, South Carolina

Please direct all correspondence and orders to:

www.southernhistoricalpress.com
or
SOUTHERN HISTORICAL PRESS, Inc.
PO BOX 1267
375 West Broad Street
Greenville, SC   29601
southernhistoricalpress@gmail.com

ISBN #0-89308-435-2

Printed in the United States of America

Many marriages which took place in Missouri prior to 1881 cannot be found in civil records. Until that year, licenses were not required. The official who performed the ceremony was enjoined to file a certificate of record within a specified period of time. Frequently he failed to do so. Distances were long, roads missing or impassable, the small fee required sometimes too much for a young frontier couple.

But newspapers have been reporting marriages in Missouri almost from the time when Joseph Charless established the Gazette in St. Louis in 1808. Weddings were news. Frequently the item included not only the couple's names but also names of parents, former residences, place where the ceremony was performed, and the person officiating. (And many thanks for the slice of cake or the glass of wine or -- on a few rare and glorious occasions -- the "little gold dollar" for the printer.)

Newspapers also frequently reported marriages of Missourians which had taken place outside of the state. Presumably, these were usually men who had become established here and gone back to marry the girls they left behind. About one-fourth of the records here are in this category.

The marriages listed here which were performed in Missouri have been checked against all available printed civil records and in some cases against the original records. It is certainly possible that some of the marriages may have been recorded in a courthouse but diligent search in several counties have failed to disclose them.

A few of these records are obviously duplicates (from two or more newspapers) but there is a variation in the names which might have provided a wrong clue. The same situation exists in a few cases where the printed record is notably different from the official record.

Some of these marriages were also certainly recorded by the church, especially the early Catholic marriages. But here again, these records are not available to the researcher unless the date and location are known; and in many cases even church records are lost or unavailable.

While many Missouri marriages are forever lost, it is hoped that this compilation will provide some answers which have previously eluded researchers.

CODE	NEWSPAPER	AREAS OF COVERAGE
BEA	St. Louis Beacon	St. Louis city and county.
BGDB	Bowling Green Democrat-Banner	Pike County and adjacent areas (Lincoln, Ralls)
BOLT	Boonslick Times	Published Fayette; covered Howard, Boone, etc.
BOMO	Missouri Register	Published Boonville (Cooper Co.) Adjacent areas.
BORE	Boonville Mo. Register	
BOWE	Western Emigrant	Boonville. These early Boonville newspapers reported from a wide area including Lafayette, Howard, Chariton, etc. as well as Cooper.
BRUNS	Brunswicker	Chariton County, some adjacent areas.
COMB	Commercial Bulletin	Boonville, Cooper County
CAMP	Plebeian	Canton. Lewis, Scotland, adjacent counties.
FREEP	Free Press	St. Louis. City and county.
FULT	Telegraph	Fulton. Callaway and adjacent counties.
GLWT	Weekly Times	Glasgow. Howard and adjacent counties.
HORL	Herald of Religious Liberty	Published in St. Louis; reported from a very large area of eastern Missouri.
INJN	Independence Journal	Jackson, Clay, Platte, etc. counties.
JEFRE	Republican	Jefferson City. Cole and adjacent counties.
INP	Independent Patriot	Jackson (Cape Girardeau Co.) An early newspaper covering a large part of southeast Missouri.
JINQ	Inquirer	Jefferson City: Cole and adjoining counties.
LEXP	Lexington Express	Lafayette Co.
MOAR	Missouri Argus	St. Louis city and county.
MIN	Missouri Intelligencer	An important early newspaper published first in Franklin, then Fayette (Howard Co.) and finally in Columbia (Boone Co.) Covered much of central Mo.
MODE	Missouri Democrat	Fayette. Howard and adjoining counties.
MOG	Missouri Gazette	The state's first newspaper (1808). Reported from the entire territory until about 1820. (St. Louis)
MORE	Missouri Republican	St. Louis. Successor to the Gazette.
MOP	Missouri Reporter	St. Louis city and county.
OSD	Old School Democrat	St. Louis, city and county.
OSIN	Osceola Independent	St. Clair and adjacent counties.
POT	Miner's Prospect	Potosi (Washington Co.) Also reported from Franklin, St. Francois, Jefferson, and other nearby counties.
PWH	Palmyra Whig	Marion and adjacent counties.
SALT	Salt River Journal	Bowling Green (Pike Co.) Also adjacent areas.
SCOMB	Commercial Bulletin	St. Louis, city and county.
SCCH	Chronotype	St. Charles and adjacent areas.
SCMO	Missourian	St. Charles and adjacent areas.
STCHMO		
SLINQ	St. Louis Inquirer	St. Louis, city and county.
SLDU	St. Louis Daily Union	" " "
SLAM	Weekly American	" " "
SOV	Shepherd of the Valley	(Catholic). Published St. Louis. Eastern Missouri.
SPAD	Springfield Advertiser	Greene and adjacent counties.
STGAZ	St. Joseph Gazette	Buchanan and adjacent counties.
SWERE	Weekly Reveille	St. Louis, city and county.
WEM	Western Emigrant	Boonville: covered Cooper and adjacent counties.
WEJO	Weston Journal	Platte and adjacent counties.
WESMO	Western Monitor	Boonville: Cooper and adjacent counties.

Some of these newspapers are located at the Missouri Historical Society, St. Louis, and the rest at the Newspaper Library of the State Historical Society of Missouri in Columbia. MOG and MORE are available in both locations.

INDEX

NOTE: the name or initials in parentheses after the name of the bride (or in some cases the groom) is that of the father.

Groom	Bride, Date and Official	Newspaper
ABBOTT, John C. of firm of Hood & Abbott, St. Louis	BREED, Lydia Maria (late Aaron) of Lynn, Mass. md. at Lynn, no date or minister given	MORE 6 Sept. 1836
ABLE, Capt. S. of St. Louis	HAILMAN, Mary Ann of and at Prairie du Rocher, IL 7th inst. by Wm. Henrie, Esq.	MORE 30 Oct. 1847
ADAMS, Wm. H. formerly Howard Co.	MYERS, Matilda A. at Chillicothe the 20th by Zadock Holcombe	BOLT 31 May 1845
ADAMS, Rudolph	TEESE, Sarah A.(John G.) of and at Frankford, Philadelphia Co. by Rev. Wm. D. Howard, the 13th	MORE 28 March 1844
ADKINSON, Samuel	MULINS, Jane at St. Louis 2 Feb. 1850 Thaddeus K. Wetmore	MORE 4 Feb. 1850
AKENS, John Lewis of St. Louis	CHASE, Chloe Marie of and at Harrisburgh no date or minister given	MORE 13 Sept. 1847
ALBRIGHT, Jacob W. of St. Louis	WILSON, Rachel of Philadelphia 22nd ult., Bishop Onderdonk	MORE 5 Aug. 1840
ALDRIDGE, Alexi of Glasgow, Mo.	PROCTOR, America of and at Danville, KY 27th, Rev. John C. Young	BOLT 14 Sept. 1844
ALEXANDER, Capt. E. B.	HOFFMAN, Amelia F. (Col.) of and at Ft. Smith, Ark. 28 Aug., Rev. D. McManus	HORL 18 Sept. 1845
ALEXANDER, Col. Walter B.	PRATTE, Theresa (Gen. Bernard) "yesterday", Rev. Niel	MORE 22 March 1824
ALLABAUGH, John R. of St. Louis	CALLAHAN, Mary Jane (Francis) at Cincinnati 17th inst., no minister given	MORE 25 Feb. 1846
ALLEN, Beverly of St. Louis	POPE, Penelope (Judge Nathaniel) of and at Kaskaskia, IL 2 Oct. 1834, Rev. Harfield	MORE 7 Oct. 1834
ALLEN, Henry of Quincy, IL	WESTCOTT, Kate A. of and at St. Louis no date given; Bishop Hawks	MORE 12 Sept. 1849

3

ALLEN, John A.　　　　　WHITE, Jane E. (Hiram)　　　MORE
of St. Louis　　　　　　at Otter Creek, IL　　　　30 Aug. 1849
　　　　　　　　　　　30 Aug., Rev. Wood

ALLEN, S. B.　　　　　　YOUNGER, Eleanor (Judge A.)　SPAD
　　　　　　　　　　　24th, Rev. J. Cathel　　　31 Dec. 1844

ALVORD, J. N.　　　　　STOWELL, Louisa　　　　　MORE
of St. Louis　　　　　　at res. A. H. Stowell, Detroit　30 Nov. 1850
　　　　　　　　　　　19th Nov., Rev. Pilcher

AMOS, W. W.　　　　　　GLEM, Emma J. (Col. Christain C.　MORE
of St. Louis　　　　　　Gleim), at Beaver Point, PA　14 April 1838
　　　　　　　　　　　27 March, Rev. Castor

ANDERSON, Dr. G. A.　　FISHER, Jemima (niece of Fred)　MORE
of Griswold City　　　　of Pinckney, Mo.　　　　　5 Nov. 1842
　　　　　　　　　　　27 Oct., Elder S. Rogers

ANDERSON, George　　　MAITLAND, Margaret J. (John, Esq.) MORE
merchant of St. Louis　　at Philadelphia　　　　　18 April 1830
　　　　　　　　　　　4 April, Bishop Kenrick

ANDERSON, Stephen　　　COLLIER, Mrs. Diana　　　　SWERE
　　　　　　　　　　　Rev. Gustavus Brown (Brurin?)　27 Sept. 1847

ANDERSON, Capt. Tom F.　IVINS, Mary S.　　　　　SWERE
　　　　　　　　　　　of Keokuk, Iowa　　　　　15 Dec. 1845
　　　　　　　　　　　29 Nov. 1845

ANDERSON, W. C., Jr.　　YEATMAN, Anna Maria (H.L.)　MORE
of St. Louis　　　　　　at Cincinnati　　　　　　25 May 1837
　　　　　　　　　　　16th inst., Rev. J. T. Brooks

ANDREWS, James L.　　　ANDREWS, Sarah Ann　　　　MODE
of Howard Co.　　　　　of Chariton Co.　　　　　4 Oct. 1847
　　　　　　　　　　　no date or minister

ANDREWS, John　　　　　SLATER, Elizabeth　　　　　MORE
　　　　　　　　　　　Wednesday, Rev. Joseph Scripps　16 Feb. 1824

ANGNEY, Capt. W. Z.　　CONKLIN, Maria A.　　　　　BRUNS
formerly of Jefferson　　of and in Santa Fe, NB(?)　7 April 1849
City　　　　　　　　　3 Feb.

ARMSTRONG, Clinton　　　LYNN, Martha P. (Wm., Esq.)　MORE
of St. Louis　　　　　　in Kingsport, TN　　　　　28 June 1847
　　　　　　　　　　　1 June, Rev. Philip Wood

ARNOLD, Thomas J.　　　TAYLOR, Louisa S., late of　MOAR
　　　　　　　　　　　Philadelphia　　　　　　11 Sept. 1835
　　　　　　　　　　　3 Sept., Rev. James Tabor

ARTHUR, John　　　　　STTARNS, Rebecca L.　　　　MORE
　　　　　　　　　　　17th, Rev. Tabor　　　　　21 June 1836

ARTHUR, John of Independence, MO	YOUNG, Ann F. (eldest dau. of Walter C., Esq.) of Jessamine Co., KY at Lexington, KY 22nd, Rev. Wm. H. Pratt	MORE 31 March 1848
ASAY, Alexander B.	LEWIS, Mary H.C. both formerly of Philadelphia, at Marion Lower College 25 Dec. 1839, Rev. H. H. Hayes	PWH 11 Jan. 1840
ASHLEY, William	CHRISTY, Eliza (William)	MORE 31 Oct. 1825
ATCHISON, John of Galena	BILLON, Emily of St. Louis "last eve" Rev. Horrell	MORE 12 May 1829
ATHEY, P.	RIFFLE, Italia 18th, Rev. Geo. A. Carroll	SLDU 21 Oct. 1846
AUD, Frances L. of Independence	THRESHLY, Emily L. of and at Louisville, KY 9th inst., Rev. McGill	INJN 31 Oct. 1844
AUSTIN, Charles H.	MACRAE, Eugenia Louisa of and at Mobile no date, by Basil Mesner, Esq.	MORE 23 Feb. 1830
AUSTIN, Wm. James of St. Louis	BOSS, Mary Ann L., formerly of Cincinnati, at Kaskaskia IL "Thurs. last" Rev. Mathews	BEA 9 Dec. 1830
AUSTIN, William J.	MORRIS, Caroline C. (James P.) 4 Sept. Rev. Tabor	MORE 9 Sept. 1834
AYRES, L. P. of White & Ayres, Warsaw	JOHNSON, Frances A. of Hartsville, in Wright Co. the 4th, minister not given	COMB 19 Nov. 1847
BABER, Hiram H. merchant of St. Charles	BOONE, Harriett M. (J.B.) of Loutre Lick, Montgomery Co. 6th, Rev. James Craig	MOG 13 Oct. 1819
BACON, Edmund G. both of St. Louis Co.	HARWOOD, Mariah Louisa Tuesday, Rev. John Brown	MORE 3 July 1831
BACON, George T., Esq. Marion (Macon?) Co.	WETMORE, Roxanna (Major) 15th inst., Rev. Griswold	MORE 17 June 1849
BADGER, Dr. Albert all of Bates Co.	HALLEY, Sarah E. at res. of Col. Halley 30 June, Rev. James Bon	OSIN 23 July 1853

BAILEY, Thompson L.   SPROULE, Martha Jane (Joseph)   MORE
of Rodney, MS   of Monroe Co.   14 July 1837
                         4 July, Rev. Samuel Briggs

BAILY, Col. David   RULAND, Susan C.   MORE
                         at Troy, Lincoln Co.   15 Oct. 1823
                         9th, no minister given

BAKER, George   HILER, Lydia (David)   INP
                        Thurs. last, Rev. Jonas(?)   (illegible ca 1822)
                           Bankson(?)

BAKER, John E.   SMITH, Dorothea (late R., Esq.) MORE
merchant, Cape Girardeau in Scott Co., the 24th   14 June 1831
Co.

BALDWIN, Robert   DUSTON, Elazema   MORE
                         Cruess, 19 Dec.   28 Dec. 1844

BALES, John   WARRANCE, Catharine K. (Wm.)   MORE
of Pittsburgh   formerly Philadelphia   2 Oct. 1839
                         30 Sept., Rev. Bernard

BALL, Albert   STIBBS, Mrs. Ellen   MORE
of Shipping Point, MO   of St. Louis   20 July 1838
                         18th, Rev. Tabor

BALL, John   CLARK, Jane, of Cape Girardeau MORE
of Chippeway Co. WI   8 Nov., Kitzmiller   9 Nov. 1850

BANNEN, Horace   BURBANKS, Elizabeth   STCHMO
(BANNER?)   15th inst., Rev. Robinson   18 April 1822

BARBER, Wm. B., Esq.   SKINNER, Nannie W.   MORE
                         1 Dec., VanCourt   4 Dec. 1847

BARNHART, John   WILSON, Ellen   MORE
                         25 Sept., D. Wetmore   26 Aug. 1843

BARR, Forrister   CALDWELL, Sarah   PWH
both of Marion Co.   at Harrison Co., KY at res.   13 April 1844
                         of Larkin Garnett, 31 March

BARRETT, J. R., Esq.   SIMPSON, Eliza F. (Hon. James) MORE
                         formerly of Westfield, KY   15 Dec. 1847
                         4 Nov., Rev. Matthews

BARRET, Wm. James   WILMANS, Mary Theodosia   MORE
formerly St. Louis   formerly Carmi, IL, at Warsaw MO 7 Oct. 1846
                         29th ult., Rev. Richard Allen

BARRON, Thomas M.   BELT, Sarah Jane V.   MORE
                         at Central Presb. Church   1 June 1850
                         30 May, Rev. Hall

BARRY, James   MULLEN, Margaret   BEA
                                     at Florissant, St. Louis Co.   10 March 1831
                                     15th, Rev. Van Nash

BARTHOLOMEW, Collins W.   SHUMATE, Elizabeth A.   BOLT
all of New Franklin,   16th, Rev. Thomas Johnson   30 Dec. 1843
Howard Co.

BARTLETT, George W.   McDOWELL, N. H.   MORE
                                     25 Sept., Cruess, JP   27 Sept.1849

BARTLETT, Joseph   CLINKINBEARD, Mary L.   MORE
                                     4th, Justice Shepard   6 April 1838

BARTON, K. L.   COLLINS, Isaetta (late John)   BOLT
                                     6th, Rev. Wm. B. Watts   15 Jan. 1842

BASEY, Henry   STIR, Ceolida   MORE
                                                                            2 Feb. 1830

BASS, John M., Esq.   GRUNDY, Miss (Felix)   MORE
of St. Louis   in Nashville   27 Jan. 1829
                                     no date or minister

BATES, Capt. David G.   POTEET, Mrs. C.   MORE
both of St. Louis   9 June 1825

BATES, Thomas Lothrop, Esq. ALEXANDER, Harriet(3rd dau. J.)   MORE
of Boston   of Johnson Co., Mo.   7 and 23 Jan.
                                     6 Dec. 1849 at Ft. Scott, KS   1850
                                     Rev. John Hale

BATTE, Mr.   ROBERTS, Miss   MOG
                                     Sat. last   24 July 1813

BATTERTON, Rev. A. R.   HALL, Ann   BRUNS
                                     at DeWitt, Carroll Co., 31st   14 June 1849

BATTU, Mr.   CHARLEVILLE, Miss   MOG
                                     no date   19 Oct. 1816

BAYFIELD, James H.   GREGG, Mary (late Thos., Esq.)   MORE
of St. Louis   of and at Baltimore MD   27 March 1840
                                     17 March, Rev. J.M. Duncan

BEACH, Milan   DREW, Mary   MORE
                                     14th, at Meth. Ch., Rev. Boyle   16 Feb. 1844

BEAL, James A., Esq.   WIDEMAN, Paty Pincke   SWERE
all of Big River,   10 April, Justice A. Brown   16 April 1849
Jefferson Co.

BEAN, James M.   RUNKLE, Frances V.   BRUNS
publisher of Paris Mercury all of Paris, Monroe Co.   28 April 1849
                                     10th, no minister given

7

BEAUFILS, Joseph   GRIMAU, Virginia (Alexander, Jr.) MORE
                          12 April, Rev. Saulnier   11 May 1830

BEEBE, E. H.   KENNETT, Caroline (P.G.)   MORE
of St. Louis   in Carrollton, IL   2 Oct. 1832
                          19th ult, Rev. Lippincott

BEEBE, Edward H.   PORTER, Frances A.   MORE
of St. Louis   at Carrollton, IL   22 March 1844
                          18 March, Rev. Barr

BEER, Capt. Henry J.   MAYNARD, Cornelia J.   MORE
of steamboat   of and at Glasgow, MO   6 Nov. 1843
Tobacco Plant   2 Nov., Rev. Calhoun

BELL, John T.   LUCKIE, Irene   MORE
of Louisiana, MO   of Louisville   15 July 1849
                          10th inst., Rev. J. W. Campbell

BELL, Joseph   FISHER, Cornelia   MORE
of St. Louis   of Jerseyville, IL   29 April 1849
                          5 April, E. J. Palmer

BELL, T. E., Esq.   HALE, E. (Judge)   MORE
                          of St. Francois Co.   11 Oct. 1850
                          6 Oct., A. H. Roberts

BELT, Henry B., Esq.   REYNOLDS, Margaret A.   SWERE
of St. Louis   of Bedford, PA at   21 Feb. 1848
                          Lewistown, IL
                          17 Feb., Rev. Steel

BELT, Dr. James Walter P. SMITH, Elizabeth   MORE
all of Benton Co.   28 March, Rev. Monroe   16 April 1847

BENNETT, Wm. M.   SHEPPARD, Nicy (John, Sen.)   INP
all of Cape Girardeau Co. 1st, Rev. T. P. Green   4 Dec. 1824

BENOIST, L. A.   HACKNEY, Esther of Mercer, PA   MORE
                          23rd inst., Rev. Lutz   27 Nov. 1832

BENOIST, Louis   BARTON, Eliza (Joseph)   MORE
of St. Louis   at Kaskaskia IL   17 Aug. 1826
                          Thurs. last.

BENOIST, Louis A.   WILSON, Sarah Elizabeth   MORE
both of this county   at Carondelet   28 Nov. 1849
                          16 Nov., Rev. Ortleib

BENOIST, S. H.   DUBOIS, Josephine (O.)   SCOMB
all of this county   yesterday, Rev. Lutz   10 July 1835

BENSON, Ira   MUNRO, Sarah (George)   BRUNS
of Trenton, MO   of Livingston Co.   20 Sept. 1849
                          13th, no minister given

8

BENSON, James R. Senior editor this paper	SKELTON, Martha A.E. Tues. last, Elder Charles Dodge	BOLT 10 May 1845
BENTON, Col. Thos. H. of St. Louis	McDOWELL, Eliza (Col.) in Rockbridge Co., VA 20 March	MOG 18 April 1821
BERRY, Henry B. of St. Louis	FAREWELL, Louisa of and at Alton, IL 15th, Lippincott	MORE 15 May 1832
BETTS, William B.	LOOMIS, Elizabeth C. at Christ Church 4 Sept., Bishop Hawks	MORE 6 Sept. 1849
BIDDLE, Maj. Thos.	MULLANPHY, Ann (John) at Florissant, St. Louis Co. 1st	MORE 10 Sept. 1823
BIGHAM, David	POND, Hannah 26th inst., Goodrich	MORE 27 June 1849
BILL, Charles merchant of St. Louis	MILLER, Elizabeth Latimer (late John), at Milton, IL 6th, Thos. Lippincott	SLINQ 15 March 1820
BILLINGS, George W.	WARREN, Elizabeth A. 9th inst., Rev. Gilbert	MORE 14 July 1846
BILLON, Charles P.	RIDDICK, Frances E. (late Col. T. F.) at Sulphur Springs, Jefferson Co. Thurs. last, Rev. Chaderton	MORE 9 Dec. 1834
BINDER, John	HOLLACHER, Appolonia 25 April, Rev. Lutz	SOV 2 May 1835
BIRGE, Henry W. of St. Louis	MEECH, Eliza W. (S. W., Esq.) at Norwich, CT 3 Sept., Rev. Boad	MORE 10 Oct.1849
BISHOP, Col. A. K.	SMITH, Mrs. Mary Tues., Rev. A. B. Curry	INJN 10 Oct. 1844
BISHOP, Martin W.	EDDY, Ann Amelia 7th inst., Justice J. B. Thomas	MORE 8 Nov. 1842
BLACKISTON, Capt. Nath'l. formerly of St. Mary's Co., MD	EACHES, Mary (only dau. of Dr.Wm.) of St. Louis Co. 29 Nov., Rev. E. C. Hutchinson, pres. at St. Peter's Chapel, Kemper College, St. Louis	MORE 1 Dec. 1842
BLACKWELL, Robert	STAPP, Malinda (late James of KY) at Kaskaskia, IL no date	SLINQ 23 Feb. 1820

BLAINE, John L.	BELL, Margaret D. (Wm., Esq.) of Allegheny 13th, Rev. James Rodgers	MORE 24 June 1844
BLAIR, Francis P., Esq. of St. Louis	ALEXANDER, Appoline(late Andrew) at Woodford Co., KY 8 Sept., Rev. Bullock	MORE 16 Sept. 1847
BLAIR, James	JOURDAN, Catharine of North St. Louis no date or minister given	MOG 8 Feb. 1817
BLAIR, John A. G. of St. Louis	MITCHELL, Elizabeth of Locust Grove, at Xenia, OH 29 Nov., Rev. Roschmiller	MORE 12 Dec. 1843
BLAIR, Montgomery	WOODBURY, Mary E. (Hon. Levi) at Portsmouth, NH 6th inst., Rev. Dr. Burroughs	MORE 21 July 1846
BLANCHARD, Benj. of St. Louis	BRADFORD, Virginia of and at Lebanon, IL 13th	MORE 14 April 1848
BLOCK, Phinehas of Pike Co.	BLOCK, Delia (Simon, Jr.) of Cape Girardeau Co. no date or minister given	INP 1 Nov. 1823
BLUE, Dr. John M. all of Bowling Green Prairie, Chariton Co.	BELL, Martha M. (Col. John M.) 4 Aug., Rev. W. H. Porter	BOLT 13 Aug. 1842
BLUNT, Charles	DEMPSTER, Adelina 9th, P. McDonald, JP	HORL 16 April 1846
BOGGS, Lilburn W. Cashier, Bank of MO	BENT, Julia Ann (Silas, Judge of Superior Court) 24th ult., Rev. Green P. Rice	MOG 2 Aug. 1817
BOGGS, LILBURN W.	BOONE, Pantha at Loutre Island, Montgomery Co.	MORE 13 Aug. 1823
BOGGS, Thomas C.	KINGSBURY, Levinia (Jere) 15th, Rev. Wm. Duncan	BOLT 19 Sept. 1846
BOGGS, Thomas J., Esq.	BARNES, Sophia (youngest dau. Shadrach) 14th, Just. Williams	MIN 23 Oct. 1824
BOGY, Louis V. of this city	PRATTE, Pelagie (late Gen. Bernard) in New York recently	MORE 2 Jan. 1837
BOLIO, Louis	RILEY, Margaret 20 Feb., D. Wetmore	MORE 21 Feb. 1844

BOON, Hampton L.

BLOY, Louisa   MIN
18th inst., Rev. Justinian Williams 24 Dec. 1822

BORDOUX, Peter

LAMBERT, Virginia   MORE
30th, Diogenes Wetmore   1 Jan. 1844

BORTON, John

COOK, Mrs. Huldah   MORE
Monday, Wright Robbens, Esq.   12 Sept. 1834

BOST, John C.

KIBBE, Harriet (2nd dau. Col. Amos) BEA
at Lewiston, Montgomery Co.   14 June 1832
31 May, Rev. A. B. Sneothen

BOSTWICK, Oliver

LaCROIX, Mrs. Julia   MORE
8 Dec.   13 Dec. 1824

BOURN, Reuben
of Palmyra

FORGVERAN, Clemency P. (John G.) PWH
in Ralls Co.   15 Jan. 1842
19 Dec. 1841; Rev. Wm. P. Cochran

BOWLES, Samuel
all of Callaway Co.

MEIER, Susanna   FULT
6th, Rev. N. Flood   8 June 1849

BOYLE, Hugh
merchant of St. Louis

HAHN, Sarah   MORE
of and at Philadelphia   31 July 1837
5th ult, Rev. Hughest

BRADEN, John

HOOD, Mary   MORE
24 Dec., Rev. Joseph R. Kerr   24 Dec. 1840

BRADY, Horace D.
formerly of Nashville, TN

LEARNED, Susan H. (Gen. J.D.)   SWERE
5 July, Rev. Alexander Vancourt   10 July 1848

BRADY, Peter

WHITE, Pauliny   MORE
3 April; Rev. H. H. Linn   4 April 1844

BRANT, Henry B.
of St. Louis

O'NEIL, Matilda   MORE
of and at Boonville, MO   16 Oct. 1849
Rev. Joseph Boyle

BRECKENRIDGE, John

POST, Eliza   MORE
recently in Bonhomme Twp.   26 May 1829
no date, no minister given

BREED, Aaron E.

BIRD, Joanna L.   MORE
18th, Rev. Hinton   20 Oct. 1843

BRENHOLTZ, J.
of St. Louis

HAMILTON, E. (eldest dau. J.G.)   MORE
formerly of Princeton NJ, at   7 Sept. 1840
Carrollton, IL
1 Sept., Rev. Woods

BRENKER, Isaac

COCK, Lucy A.   BRUNS
in Howard Co., 31 May   8 June 1848

BRICE, Lt. B.W.	KETCHUM, Eliza E. (late Maj. of 6th Inf.) at Jefferson Barracks 28th, Rev. Horrell	MORE 10 May 1831
BRIGGS, Ebenezer	BENTON, Mary T. 29 March, Rev. Bullard	MORE 30 March 1848
BRIGGS, Thomas of St. Louis	ALLINGTON, Mary of Marine Settlement, IL 28 March, Rev. Lippincott	MORE 1 April 1844
BRIGHT, George Y. late of Lexington, KY	DeLAURIER, Susan C.A.F. (Charles F.) Thurs. last	MOG 11 Dec. 1818
BRIGHT, Capt. Josiah	TESSON, Mrs. Eliza Sun. last, Rev. DeAndreis	MOG 2 June 1819
BROADDUS, W.H.C., Esq.	DUDLEY, Anne Virginia Thurs. last, Rev. Hurley	PWH 24 Dec. 1846
BROOKS, Edward druggist of St. Louis	RIDDICK, Virginia C.(late Col.T.F.) at Sulphur Springs, Jefferson Co. Thurs. last, Rev. Chaderton	MORE 9 Dec. 1834
BROWN, Andrew J. formerly of VA	SHORE, Sarah W. of Osage Co. 17th ult., Miles T. Jennings, JP	MORE 13 Dec. 1842
BROWN, Azariah	HAYS, Joanah Charette Twp., Montgomery Co. 14 March, Douglass Wyatt	SCMO 18 April 1822
BROWN, Dr. Benj. B. of St. Louis	RITTER, Eliza R.A. of Nassau, New Providence at Philadelphia 28 August, Bishop Onderdonk	MORE 12 Sept. 1834
BROWN, Clement	JAMES, Rebecca (James)	MORE 17 May 1824
BROWN, John of St. Charles	HOWELL, Nancy (John) of St. Charles 13th, Rev. Craig	MOG 26 April 1820
BROWN, Joseph of St. Louis	STEPHENSON, Martha of and at Prince Edward Co. VA	MORE 31 May 1827
BROWN, Livingston	CLARK, Anne E. (Gen. John B.) Thurs., Wm. Monroe	BOLT 5 Dec. 1846
BROWN, Morgan W. of St. Louis	HEADENBOURG, Emily Jane of and at Monticello, Madison Co., IL 5 Sept., Rev. Wm. Holmes	SWERE 17 Sept. 1848

BROWN, Robert all of Howard Co.	VENABLES, Matilda	MIN 5 March 1821
BROWN, Thomas formerly Washington, PA	BAILEY, Mary L. 4th, Rev. Hutchinson	MORE 6 May 1848
BROWN, William all of Clay Co.	BAXTER, Lydia on board Steamboat <u>Pirate</u> 30 Nov., Rev. Wallace	MORE 6 Dec. 1837
BROWNELL, Isaac W. of St. Louis	BROWN, Lucia Emelie (only dau. of W. A. Esq.) of Adamsville, RI at Christ Church, Hartford, CT 17 January	MORE 11 Feb. 1850
BUFORD, Dr. Merry of Missouri	DIMMITT, Catharine G. of Mason Co., KY 25th ult.	MORE 10 April 1840
BURBBYGE, J. B. of St. Louis	WELDIN, Mary C. of and at Pittsburgh 18 July, Rev. Joel Dolby, Jr.	MORE 30 July 1839
BURCKHARTT, Matthias N.	JACKSON, Julia Ann (Maj. Thomas) Thurs. last	MODE 22 Nov. 1847
BURD, John W.	GOODFELLOW, Eliza Ann (John) 13th, Rev. Tabor	MORE 14 Aug. 1842
BURKE, John	MOORE, Mary E. (Capt.) 9 March, Rev. John C. Lynd	MORE 11 March 1846
BURNBANKS, Elijah	RENNOLDS, Nancy Sunday last	MIN 1 Oct. 1822
BURNETT, George Jr.	FORDER, Sarah Anna at Jefferson Barracks 7 Nov., McCarty, Chaplain	MORE 9 Nov. 1850
BURNHAM, Foster	TODD, Elizabeth 9th inst., Rev. Edw. Turner	MIN 17 Dec. 1822
BURRESS, Samuel	GENTRY, Martha Boone Co. 13 May, Rev. C. Gentry	MIN 22 May 1830
BURRISS, Davenport	CASON, Ann E. (Geo.) 1st inst.	MODE 26 July 1847
BUSTIN, David	VACHARD, Genevieve 23rd, Rev. Lutz	SOV 25 March 1835
BUTLER, John	FOURT, Margaret 14 March, Hugh McDermid, J.P.	SCMO 18 April 1822

13

BUTTERFIELD, Francis A. of Louisville	MARCIA, Francis E. 17th, J. P. Kitzmiller	MORE 18 Oct. 1848
BUTTS, John	McCULLOH, Ann at res. D. L. Rizer Thurs. last, Rev. Williams	MORE 2 Sept. 1843
BYLAND, Edward M. Esq. of St. Louis	WAYFIELD, Anne Eliza (Dr. Elisha) at Fayette Co., KY, Christ Church 19 Nov., Rev. Berkeley	MORE 23 Nov. 1850
BYRNE, Michael	CARROLL, Katherine (Lawrence) Mon. last	MORE 8 Oct. 1823
CADY, Cyril C., Esq. of Palmyra	SAVAGE, Mary G.(Alexander) of Bangor, ME at res. of her brother in Quincy, IL 3 July, Rev. Marks	PWH 6 July 1844
CAIN, Jacob M.	McALISTER, Eliza Jane 13th inst., Justice McKenney	MORE 14 Feb. 1846
CALDWELL, Larkin G. of Marion Co.	MARTIN, Nancy (Col. John) of Ralls Co. at Capt. Wilson's near Frankfort, KY, 2 April	PWH 13 April 1844
CALLAHAN, Henry C. of Platte Co.	METCALF, Sarah (Alfred) of and at Walnut Hills, Ohio; formerly Fleming Co., KY 4th, Rev. Saml. Wilson	MORE 12 Jan. 1844
CAMP, Hiram	EADS, Polly at Camp Branch, Warren Co., MO 26? July	MORE 29 July 1837
CANOLE, Col. Charles of Howard Co.	KAVANAGH, Mrs. of Boone Co. 19th inst.	MIN 27 Sept. 1827
CAPLES, Rev. W. G.	BAYLEY, Mrs. Julia E. (dau. Dr. M. C. Spencer) 13th, at M.E. Church	BRUNS 27 Sept. 1849
CARLILE, Stephen both formerly of Cincinnati	POOLE, Ann 29th ult, Rev. Tombs	MORE 1 July 1848
CARLISLE, Capt. John	ROBERTSON, Mrs. Eliza 17th inst., 4th St. M.E. Church, Rev. J. Boyle	MORE 19 March 1844
CARR, Wm. C. Judge Circuit Court	BENT, Dorcas (late Silas, Esq.) Thurs., Rev. Potts	MORE 15 Dec. 1829

CARROLL, Chas. C., Esq.   BELT, Sarah E. (late Dr. F.T.)   MORE
of St. Louis   of Botetourt Co., Va., at   11 Aug. 1848
   home of her mother in
   Lebanon, IL   9th inst

CARSON, Henry S.   ROBARDS, Martha Ann   SWERE
   17 Dec.   28 Dec. 1846

CARSON, John B.   SMITH, Ann   MORE
   26 Dec., Rev. Bernard   30 Dec. 1843

CARTER, Eli   FORD, Jane   MORE
of St. Louis   of Rocheport   27 Dec. 1850
   17 Dec.

CARTER, John F.   BROOKHART, Ann Cecelia (David)   MORE
of Weston, MO   of Jefferson Co., KY, formerly   8 Nov. 1844
   of Boonesboro, MD
   31st, Rev. Miller

CARTER, Rinaldo S.   COOPER, Sallie H.   MORE
both formerly of New Jersey   Rev. J. N. Arnett   1 Aug. 1850

CARUTHERS, Samuel, Esq.   SMITH, Sophronia   MORE
of Fredericktown, MD   of and at Greenville, MO   29 April 1849
   19th inst., Rev. David Bullock

CASEY, James   PLANT, Nancy   MORE
   13th, A. Wetmore   14 Sept. 1844

CASSILY, P.   McKENNEY, Mary Ann   MORE
of St. Louis   of and at Cincinnati   7 Dec. 1830
   18th, Rev. Dr. Jullen

CASTLEMAN, W. S.   JOHNSON, Amanda (Jacob, Esq.)   MORE
of St. Louis   of and in Independence   8 Jan. 1849
   28 Dec., Rev. Thos. Ashby

CAUGHLIN, David   BEALL, Ellen (E.)   MORE
of St. Louis   of and at Alton, IL   17 Feb. 1844
   8th inst., Rev. Bastian

CAULK, Isaac   ORR, Mrs. M.   MORE
both of Bonhomme Twp.   22nd, Henry McCullough   30 March 1830

CHAMBERS, A. B.   CARR, Mrs. Elizabeth   MORE
of Bowling Green, MO   late of Troy, MO   19 Nov. 1833
   at Thomas Dudley's near
   Lexington, KY, 28 Oct.

CHANDLER, Samuel B.   LaCROIX, Adeline   MORE
   at res. of George Reynolds   27 Jan. 1834
   21st inst., Rev. P.J. Doutreligne(?)

CHAYTOR, Joseph   SNODGRASS, Theresa (Isaac)   SWERE
   25 Nov., Rev. Pollock   29 Nov. 1847

CHEEK, William   PULLIAM, Ann   MIN
                            in Saline Co.   31 Dec. 1822
                            17th inst., Rev. Ebenezer Rogers

CHENAULT, Wm. M.   SHANNON, Emily C. (Thomas)   SPAD
                            in Newton Co.   11 July 1846
                            3 June, Rev. Patterson

CHILDS, Benjamin Franklin BROWN, Ellen   MORE
of Illinois   of St. Louis   23 Aug. 1836
                           17th, Rev. Tabor

CHILDS, Caleb   KING, Ann   MORE
                          23rd, Rev. Hinson   25 Jan. 1843

CHISM, Howard   EMBRY, Mrs. Sarah   WEM
of Versailles, Morgan Co. (Isaac Duncan of Cooper)   8 Aug. 1839
                          31 July, Rev. S. C. Davidson

CHOUTEAU, Francis   MENARD, Theresse B. (Lt. Gov.)   MOG
of St. Louis   of and at Kaskaskia, IL   28 July 1819
                          12th, Rev. Desmoulin

CHOUTEAU, Paul L.   DUBREUIL, Constance   MOG
(son Major Pierre)   (dau. Mme. Vve.   6 March 1813

CHOUTEAU, Paul L.   HAY, Aurora (John)   BEA
of St. Louis   of and at Belleville, IL   11 Nov. 1830
                          3rd inst.

CHOUTEAU, Peter, Jr.   GRATIOT, Emile   MOG
                          16 June   24 July, 1813

CHRISTMAN, Wm.   BIRON, Eliza   MORE
                         (niece of Joseph Bouju)   26 April 1824
                         yesterday, Rev. Niel

CLAFLIN, William   HARDING, Nancy   MORE
of St. Louis   of Hopkinton, MA   4 Nov. 1840
                         Wed. last, at house of Silas Simon
                         Rev. Jno. H. Haywood

CLAFLIN, William   DAVENPORT, Mary   MORE
of St. Louis   of and at Hopkinton, MA   27 Feb. 1845
                         12 Feb., Rev. John Webster

CLARDY, Dr. E. S.   LONG, Mary E. (William)   MORE
of Farmington, MO   of Gravois Twp., St. Louis Co.   2 Sept. 1848
                         at Ste. Genevieve
                         22nd, Rev. Headlee

CLARK, Bennett H.   TRIGG, Susannah (Col. Stephen)   MIN
                         late of Estill Co., KY   18 March 1820
                         in Howard Co., last Thurs.

16

CLARK, Henry   CHILDS, Ellen Ann (Thos., Esq.)   MORE
both of St. Louis   20 Nov., Rev. J. T. Tucker   23 Nov. 1838

CLARK, J. K.   GLASGOW, M.S.   MORE
    8th inst., Bishop Hawks   11 May 1849

CLARK, Capt. John B.   SANFORD, Henrietta C.   MORE
3rd Reg.U.S.Inf.   (Alexander) of Baltimore, MD   8 Dec. 1829
    Wed., Rev. Horrell

CLARK, John C.   LEWIS, Agnes W. (S. Walker)   MORE
of St. Louis   at Monticello, Howard Co.   1 Aug. 1844
    25 July, A. D. Corbin

CLARK, William G.   MILLER, Julia   MORE
of St. Louis   of and at Baltimore, MD   13 Oct. 1840
    1 Oct., Rev. Morris

CLARKE, Wm. H.   PHILLIPSON, Amanda   MORE
of Chicago   of St. Louis   30 March 1839
    at Ft. Howard, Green Bay
    28 Feb., Rev. Ames

CLARKSTON, Caleb   RAY, Mary Ann   MORE
    25 April, D. Wetmore   26 April 1844

CLARY, R. E.   PHILIPSON, Esther (J.)   MORE
U. S. Army   Tues. last, Rev. Saulnier   7 April 1829

CLELAND, Beriah   GRIFFITH, Polly   MORE
of St. Louis   of Bonhomme Twp.   14 June 1827
    7th, at Henry Walton's
    by Rev. Salmon Giddings

CLINTON, Charles D.   FARIS, Catherine   MORE
    Rev. Salmon Giddings   14 March 1825

CLOUSE, George   MILLER, Sydney   MORE
    23 July, I.B. Thomas, JP   25 July 1844

CLUFF, Samuel   CARSON, Martha Jane (oldest of   PWH
of LaGrange, Lewis Co.   Capt. Wm.) Tues. last, Lewis Co.   6 May 1847
    Rev. John Keach

COATS,Alfred A.   WARREN, Margaret   MIN
    16th ult., Howard   5 Nov. 1822

COCHRAN, Marshall Stark   JANUARY, Mary   MORE
    30 June, B. Johnston, JP   1 July 1847

COCK, Wm. M.   BROWN, Mary Fletcher (Rev.Rich.G.)BRUNS
of Chariton Co.   of Campbell Co. VA   9 Sept.1847

17

COE, Alven | MARKS, Elizabeth (David) | MOG
at Milton, IL | 10 March 1819
25th, T. G. Davison, Esq.

COFER, Thos. A. | SMARR, Susan F. | MODE
formerly Bedford Co., VA | 11 March | 21 March 1847

COGSWELL, Oscar B. | SHAFFNER, Elenora | MORE
9th, Rev. Griswold | 10 June 1846

COHEN, Albert B. | OWINGS, Sarah (I.W.) | SWERE
formerly of Baltimore, MD | 22 Dec. 1845
22 Dec.

COLE, Dr. David V. | FLEISCHMAN, Henrietta A. | SWERE
of Iowa | of St. Louis | 12 March 1849
10 March, Bishop Hawks

COLE, John | WALKER, Sarah Ann | POT
12 Sept., Washington Co. | 20 Sept. 1849

COLEMAN, Samuel | LEWIS, Mary Catherine | PWH
28 May, Rev. Marvin | 8 June 1848

COLLIER, George | BELL, Sarah Ann (Wm.) | MORE
of St. Louis | of Pittsburgh, at Allegheny Town | 15 Oct. 1838
4th inst.

COLLINS, Morris | TUTHILL, Mary S. (late Selah) | MORE
of St. Louis | of New Haven, CT | 28 Aug. 1847
at Rev. Spring's Church, NYC
18th inst, Rev. Chapman

COLWELL, S. S. | LA CHARITY, Mary | MORE
of Mississippi | 29th inst., Rev. Gazell | 30 May 1849

CONNELL, Wm. Fletcher | HOPKINS, Sarah A.D. of and | MORE
of St. Louis | at Washington, D.C. | 26 Sept. 1849
16 Sept., Rev. Chas. Davis

CONROY, James | STRACZER, Mrs. Mary | PWH
of Hannibal | of Palmyra at Quincy IL | 11 May 1844
Rev. Tucker

CONNELLY, William W. | KIZER, Elizabeth S. | MORE
14 May, Rev. Jos. Boyle | 15 May 1850

CONSTER, George | ENGLISH, Patsy (Thomas) | INP
of Perry Co. | of Cape Girardeau Co. | 1 March 1823
20th inst., Rev. John Harbison

CONWAY, F. R. | COLLINS, Martha L. | MORE
Recorder Land Titles St.L. | of and at Howard County | 2 June 1836
at res. John Ball
18th, Rev. John Y. Staernes

COOK, Hon. Daniel P. Rep. Congress (IL?)	EDWARDS, Julia (Hon. Ninian) 7th,	MOG 16 May 1821
COOK, John of Waynesville, MO	WALTON, Evy D. (Moses, Esq.) of Gasconade Co. 3 Sept., Thos. Taylor, Esq.	MORE 24 Sept. 1840
COOK, Robert of St. Louis	SHANNON, Adeline B. of and at Philadelphia, Grace Church 2nd inst., Rev. Wm. Suddards	MORE 6 March 1848
COOKE, Lt. Philip St. George U.S. Army	HERTZOG, Rachel W. af Ft. Leavenworth at home of Major Dougherty 28th ult., Rev. Edwards	MORE 16 Nov. 1830
COOLY, Martin	ALDRICH, Louisa M. 7th inst., Rev. Townsend	MORE 9 Nov. 1848
COONS, Dr. A. J.	FICKLIN, Frances Marshall (George, Esq.) of Culpeper, VA at Washington City 24 Feb.	MORE 18 March 1846
COOPER, Benjamin of Howard Co.	GALBRETH, Martha of Saline Co. 20th ult, Eb. Rodgers	MIN 10 Aug. 1826
COPELAND, Thomas	HOWIS, Mary 29 Jan., Winright	MORE 31 Jan. 1845
COPELIN, John R.	WILSON, Jane M.D. of Ralls Co., formerly of Carlisle, PA at res. Matthew L. Caruthers 4 June, Rev. Jesse Green	PWH 11 June 1842
COPES, Thomas P.	CERE, Mary at Portage des Sioux Saturday	SCMO 12 Sept. 1822
CORBIN, Abel R.	McALISTER, Elizabeth at St. Louis 11 June, Rev. Drummond	MIN 20 June 1835
CORNELIUS, James	COPHER, Sarah 23 March?	MIN 7 April 1826
COSGREAVE, Moses	CLEARY, Mrs. Ann 12th, Rev. Dubourg	MOG 18 Oct. 1820
COURTENAY, Thomas E. of St. Louis	CLENDENIN, Minnie (eld.J.M.) of St. Louis at Farmington, Jefferson Co., KY 25 Aug., Rev. Leacock	MORE 30 Aug. 1847

COURTOIS, Joseph   CHOUQUETTE, Eulalie   MORE
                          24 Jan. in Carondelet   9 Feb. 1826

COURTOIS, Louis   ROBERT, _____   MORE
                          23 Jan. in Carondelet   9 Feb. 1826

COWLES, William P.   KIRBY, Sarah R.   MORE
of wt. Louis   at Bainbridge, NY   14 Sept. 1844
                          29th, Rev. Goodrich

COX, William   BELTZHOOVER, Elizabeth   MORE
of St. Louis   of and at Pittsburgh   7 Sept. 1830
                          12 Aug., Rev. E. P. Swift

COZENS, Horatio   SANGUINET, Carolina (late Charles) MOG
                                                       27 Nov. 1818

CRAIG, Rev. James   BOONE, Delinda (Major Nathan) MOG
of St. Charles   of and at Femme Osage, St. Chas. 12 May 1819
                          29 April, Rev. Peck

CRAIG, John   BARGER, Amelia (Jasper)   MIN
of Callaway   of and at Boone Co.   21 April 1832
                          12 April, Rev. D. Doyle

CRAIG, Josiah C.   MOORE, Martha Isabella   MORE
                          (old. dau. James of Scott Co.KY) 8 March 1843
                          22nd ult, Rev. John Gano

CRAWFORD, David   GARDNER, Elizabeth   PWH
                          23 June, Rev. Richard Sharp 2 July 1842

CRAWFORD, Thomas L.   ROBINSON, Mary (late Henry) MORE
                          of Jefferson Co.   1850
                          at "Grub Alley Castle"
                          1 June, Rev. T. W. Capers

CREWS, Dr. Samuel   WARD, Elizabeth (Wm., Esq.) MIN
                          Howard Co.   7 March 1828
                          Thurs. last, Rev. John Bull

CRISSWELL, Capt. George   ALLISON, Statyra   MORE
of Washington Co.   in St. Louis   21 Dec. 1846
                          15 Dec., Rev. John P. Cowan

CROOKS, Ramsay   PRATTE, Emilia (eld. Bernard) MORE
of New York   14 March 1825

CROPPER, Levin, Esq.   BAILEY, Mary, widow   MORE
of Cooper Co.   at her res. in Monroe Co.IL(?) 5 Dec. 1838
                          16 Nov., Duthiel Converse, Esq.

CROSLER, Henry   LOPER, Sarah (Col. James)   MORE
                          Thursday, Rev. Horrell   22 Jan. 1833

CROSMAN, Lt. G.H. U. S. Army	FOSTER, H.B. at Jefferson Barracks 2nd, Rev. Horrel	MORE 7 April 1829
CULTON, D. M. of Washington Co.	POLK, Eveline M. Howard Co. 20th, Elder W.W.Burton	BOLT 29 May 1841
CUMMINS, H. F. of Weston, MO	STEVENS, Eliza J. of and at Paris, TN 19 March, Rev. Warren	MORE 2 April 1844
CUNIFFE, John B. of St. Louis	BALLARD, Mrs. Mary of New Jersey 18 Jan., Rev. C. Deleroux	MORE 5 Feb. 1849
CUNNINGHAM, Jos. all of Randolph Co.	GOODING, Mary Jane Thurs., Rev. Saml. E. Davis	BOLT 14 Nov. 1846
CURTIS, Charles H. of Tennessee	MULDROW, Ellen (James) of this county, in Iowa Terr. 2nd inst.	PWH 17 Feb. 1844
CUTHBERT, Samuel	JONES, Eugenia B. (C.G.) 25 May, Bishop Hawks	MORE 30 May 1848
CUTRER, Isaac W.	DUNNICA, America V. (Judge) of this city, at Covington, LA 11th, Rev. Lee	JEFRE 2 April 1842
DADE, John, Esq. of Boonville, MO	RECTOR, Mrs. Eliza S. at Jacksonville, IL 1 May	MIN 24 May 1834
DAGGET, John D. Merchant of St. Louis	SPARKS, Sarah Sun. last, Rev.Giddings	MOG 7 Feb. 1821
DALRYMPLE, Wallace of St. Louis	THORBURN, Jessie (eld. Geo.C.) New York, 23 Sept.	MORE 7 Oct. 1844
DALY, James of Chariton	MEDLEY, Sarah 20 May, Rev. S.C. Davis	MIN 5 June 1830
DALY, John	FENNINGTON, Hesta 13 Dec., Rev. Field	MORE 15 Dec. 1843
DALY, Michael	TIMON, Rosa T. M. (James, mecht.) Thurs. last, Bishop Dubourg	MOG 1 Sept. 1819
DARNES, William P.	LAUCHLIN, Mary Jane (late James) of Scott Co. 19th	HORL 11 Sept. 1845
DASHIELL, Alfred H., Jr. of St. Louis	MASON, Mary Murray (Jno. E., Esq.) in New York 27 Sept., Rev. Thos. H. Skinner	MORE 7 Oct. 1848

DAVIDSON, John C.	TALBOT, Sophia (Dr. James) of Loutre Island 18th, Rev. Wm. Stevens	MORE 22 Jan. 1842
DAVIS, Henry H. both of Chariton Co.	CRAWLEY, Elizabeth Ann 4th, Rev. Jesse Green	BOLT 8 Jan. 1842
DAVIS, Robert T.	GAULDING, Mary Saline Co., 24th	BRUNS 7 June 1849
DAVIS, Rolla	NORRIS, Mrs. Maria (widow of Robert N.), late of Culpeper Co., VA, at Jefferson City 3rd, Rev. Pierce	BOWE 10 Jan. 1839
DAWSON, John of St. Louis	CLARK, Lucy L. of Mt. Pleasant, MO 16 May, Rev. Jos. Tabor	MORE 18 May 1842
DAY, Franklin O. of St. Louis	AULL, Lavinia at St. Paul's Church, Steubenville, OH	MORE 4 Oct. 1849
DEAN, George B. of Brooklyn	DeFOREST, Ellen Jane Sat. last, Rev. Tabor	MOAR 23 Oct. 1835
DEAN, Henry C.	SAPPINGTON, Margaret B.(Richard) late of Gravois, at Madison Co., IL, 13 Oct., Rev. Bullard	MORE 15 Oct. 1844
DEAN, Capt. James U.S. Army	CHRISTY, Harriet (Maj. Wm.) of this county Thurs., Rev. Horrell	MORE 12 Jan. 1830
DEAN, Thomas A. of St. Louis	MacDONALD, Jennie at Steubenville, OH 29 Nov., Rev. Cummings	MORE 8 Dec. 1850
DeBRUEN, John	SPROUT, Mrs. Mary Rev. Joel Haden, elder C.C.	SPAD 1 Aug. 1844
DE CAMPS, Wm., Esq. of Wellsburgh, VA	WISHART, Jane B. (Dr. James) in Wheeling, VA 21 June, Rev. Wallace	MORE 7 Aug. 1847
DE GUIRE, Benjamin	ISOM, Marcelite 19 Feb. 1833	SOV 9 March 1833
DeHODIAMONT, _____	KEATEN, Mary 10 April, Rev. Borgna	SOV 20 April 1833
DE LA COSSITT, H. Editor Hannibal "Gazette"	JACOBS, Jane A. (late John) Rev. Jacob Sigler	PWH 17 Feb. 1848

22

DeLASSUS, Lnon	ELLIOTT, Mary Lewis (late Maj. Henry) at res. Col. Jos. D. Grafton, Ste. Genevieve 19th inst., Rev. Dalu___?	MORE 26 Sept. 1837
DEWEES, Nimrod of Jacksonville, IL	TALBOT, Mary J. of Fayette 24th, Rev. Hopson	MORE 29 July 1848
DEVRICKS, John	MORTON, _____(Samuel) Tues. last	PWH 24 Dec. 1846
DEWEY, Walter	HISENOGGLE, Hannah Jefferson Co. 10 Oct., Rev. John Buren	MORE 9 Oct. 1839
DEWITT, A. B.	CROMWELL, Mary of Gravois 13th, Rev. Giddings	MORE 27 Dec. 1827
DILLON, P. M. of Reily & Dillon	EADS, Eliza Jane 28 Jan., Rev. Lutz	MORE 6 Feb. 1836
DINKLE, James M. all of Saline Co.	RICHESON, Julia E. 19th	BRUNS 23 Dec. 1847
DINNIES, John C. of St. Louis	SHACKELFORD, Anna Peyre (late W. F.) of and at Charleston, SC	MORE 1 June 1830
DIX, Edw. H.	POGUE, Mary Jane late of Baltimore Thurs. last, Bishop Hawks	HORL 14 May 1846
DORWART, David	SNYDER, Anna Maria of Lancaster, PA, 18 Feb.	MORE 9 March 1847
DOSSETT, Henry L.	BLACKBURN, Georgianna (Capt.) late of Kentucky, in St.L.Co. 3 Sept., Bishop Hawks	MORE 7 Sept. 1846
DOUGHERTY, John	HERTZOG, Mary (Joseph) Rev. Giddings, no date	MORE 26 Nov. 1823
DOUGHTY, James W. of St. Louis	NICHOLLS, Margaret (Wm. S., Esq.) of and at Georgetown, DC 13th ult.	MORE 2 March 1840
DOUGLASS, Thompson	BISSELL, Cornelia (Gen. Danl.) Tues. last, Hon. David Barton	MOG 27 Sept. 1817
DOWDALL, Robert W.	JOHNSON, Margaret 18th inst., Rev. Linn	MORE 23 March 1849

DOWNS, Wm. L. L. all of Linn Co.	JACKSON, Martha Ann 9th	BRUNS 18 Nov. 1848
DOWTHIT, Green L. of Morgan Co.	TURNER, Sally Ann (James) of this county Rev. Turner	BOLT 17 April 1841
DOYLE, Michael of Missouri	LIGHTFOOT, Mrs. Susan at Cincinnati 13 June, Rev. J. E. Wilson	MORE 21 June 1844
DRAPER, Daniel of Louisiana, MO	RIGGS, Julia of Lincoln Co. 14 April, Rev. J.W. Hopkins	MORE 29 April 1840
DRIPS, Charles A. of <u>Kansas</u>, MO	McCONAPY, Eliza of St. Louis 18 March, Rev. Morris	MORE 22 March 1850
DRUILLARD, Louis of St. Louis	DANIELS, Mary E. (late Wm.) of Hamilton, OH in "Peru" 5 Sept., Rev. McClelland	MORE 14 Sept. 1850
DRYDEN, John D.S., Esq. of Palmyra	WINCHELL, Sarah M. (Col. E.) at Greenfield 15 March, Rev. J. Blatchford	PWH 19 March 1842
DRYDEN, John D.S.	BARR, Sarah (Rev. Joseph) of Newark, Del., at res. A. F. Barr 15 April, Rev. Hayes	PWH 22 April 1847
DuBOIS, C. of St. Louis	BENJAMIN, Sarah (Ira, Esq.) of and in New York City 20th ult, Rev. Jno. S. Ebaugh	MORE 3 Feb. 1848
DUGAN, Robert	CUNNINGHAM, Caroline, at res. E.C. Cunningham, St. Charles 28 Oct., Rev. James Green	SCCH 9 Nov. 1850
DeMUN, Mr._____	GRATIOT, Isabelle (ygst. Charles) Tues. last	MOG 4 April 1812
DENNY, Lt. St. Clair	HAMILTON, Caroline Frances (Major T.) at Prairie du Chien IL	MORE 10 Jan. 1825
DESHLER, David	TAYLOR, Ellen 17 March	MORE 21 March 1845
DETCHEMENDY, Julius A.	MALOTT, Edna Maria 12 April, Rev. Bernier	SWERE 16 April 1849
DETHIER, Louis	HEMPSTEAD, Mrs. Clarisa C. Thurs., Bishop Dubourg	MOG 22 Sept. 1819

DUHRING, Andrew
Merchant, late of Phila.

PRIMM, Mary A.
16th, Rev. Lutz

MORE
18 June 1836

DUNKLIN, James, Esq.

COOLY, Lucinda
of Jefferson Co.
13 Feb., Rev. Lyons

MORE
20 Feb. 1845

DUNLAVY, Richard

CARTMILL, Mrs. Maria
Thurs., Rev. James E. Welch

MOG
24 May 1820

DUVAL, Richard M.
formerly of Cincinnati

DeLAURIERE, Clarisse Ozite F.
(Charles F.)
21st, Rev. Dubourg

MOG
27 Jan. 1819

DWYER, William J.

CANTON, Eliza
of and at New Orleans
12 June

MORE
21 June 1847

DYER, William F.
of St. Louis

HUGGINS, Julia A. (F.) of
Liberty
17 Nov., Rev. T. M. Bacon

STJGZ
22 Nov. 1845

DYON, P. H. Leblanc
formerly of Canada

JARVAIS, Josephin
4th inst., Bishop Kenrick

MORE
6 Jan. 1848

EAGER, John M.
Counselor at law

FISH, Jane Maria (Thos. F., Esq.)
of Newburgh, NY
26th ult, Rev. John Johnston

MORE
8 Aug. 1843

EATON, Hon. John H.

TIMBERLAKE, Mrs. Margaret
at Washington

MIN
6 Feb. 1829

EDMONDSON, Julius

PARKER, America
in Jackson Co.
19 March, Rev. Wm. Parker

LEXP
25 March 1845

EDWARDS, Dorsson
late Cincinnati

HELLER, Harriet Caroline (John)
formerly VA
Thurs., Rev. Davis

MORE
9 Nov. 1830

EDWARDS, Joseph R.
of St. Louis

CHAMBERLAIN, Mary
of and at Springdale, OH
21 March, Rev. Aten

MORE
29 March 1839

EDWARDS, Nelson G.
of St. Louis

COOPER, Harriet J.
at Alton, IL
7 Oct., Rev. Herrell

SLDU
12 Oct. 1846

EIDSON, Newton

BLESSING, Susan
Tues. last, Rev. C. A. Leaman

CAMP
16 June 1848

ELDER, Lewis P.

ABEL, Susan (Robert)
of Ralls Co.
13th, Rev. Cusick

PWH
22 April 1847

25

ELLET, John G.
SKILLMAN, Mary Jane (late Andrew) MORE
of Baton Rouge 9 Aug. 1848
8 Aug., Bishop Hawks

ELLINGTON, Wm.
RICHARDSON, Betsy (John) MORE
of Gravois Twp., St.L.Co. 17 Nov. 1829
1st, P. Ferguson, Esq.

ELLIOT, Rev. Wm. G., Jr.
of St. Louis
CRANCH, Abby Adams (Hon. Wm.) MORE
29 June, Philadelphia 14 July 1837

ELY, Dr. Ezra Stiles
of Missouri
HOLMES, Caroline MORE
of Philadelphia at Abingdon PA 13 July 1843
9 June

EMANUEL, Isaac
DeHAAN, Anney MORE
3 Dec., A. Wetmore 5 Dec. 1844

EMBREE, Jas. H.
TREGASKIS, Elizabeth Anne MORE
2 July, Rev. Linn 4 July 1848

EMERSON, John S.
of St. Louis
DUFFEY, Louisa M. (G.H.) MORE
Alexandria, VA 11 Sept. 1847
31 Aug., Rev. Gillias

EMGE, Peter
HAPPT, Anna Mary MOAR
20 March, Justice Sheppard 29 March 1839

EMMERSON, Alexander R.
ROMINE, Amanda MORE
11th inst., Squire Sweeney 18 Oct. 1848

ENGELS, Nathaniel
BROWN, Christina MOAR
Monday last, P. Walsh, Esq. 9 Sept.1836

ENGLISH, James Lawrence
of St. Louis
WORTHINGTON, Martha Augusta MORE
(Edward) form. Mercer Co., KY 26 March 1836
of and at Rushville,Schuyler Co. IL
15th

ENNIS, William
BERRY, Sarah Jane, at home of BEA
Col. Wm. Berry, River des Peres, 24 Feb. 1831
St. Louis Twp., St.L.Co
17th, Rev. Thos. R. Musick

EVANS, Augustus H.
JAMES, Mildred MORE
9th inst. 6 July 1826

EVANS, John P.
of St. Louis
ROMANS, Catherine B. MORE
at Pavoula, NJ 17 Aug. 1850
6 Aug., Rev. Paul Van Clief

EWING, E. B., Esq.
both of Ray Co.
ALLEN, Elizabeth A. LEXP
at res. Dr. Thos. Allen 24 June 1845
Rev. T. J. Simpson

EWING, R. C.   HARRIS, Maria Louisa   JINQ
of Richmond   (Capt. Thomas)   2 Dec. 1840
                         at Rock Hill, MD
                         9 Nov., Rev. Jones

FARMER, N.   SUMMERVILLE, Nancy G.,   PWH
                         late of Palmyra; in Dade Co. 30 March 1848
                         Rev. J. D. Montgomery

FARNESWORTH, Alden   WILLIAMS, Abigail   SCMO
                         on the Dardenne, 27 Dec.   3 Jan. 1822
                         Rev. Charles S. Robinson

FARNHAM, Russell   BOSSERON, Susan   MORE
                         Tues., Rev. Saulnier   3 Nov. 1829

FARRIS, Robert P.   BOWEN, Eliza Seymore (eld.   MORE
                         of Aaron S., Esq.) of Cincinnati 9 Aug. 1848
                         3rd inst., Rev. Rice

FARWELL, Abel G.   BARTLETT, Susan Walker (Levi, Esq.) MORE
of St. Louis   at Boston 12th inst.   25 Dec. 1844

FASSEU, Louis Ignace   LEFAVRE, Phillippine M.   MORE
   Antoine of Dunquerque, of Neufchatel, Switzerland   22 Sept. 1829
   North. Dept. France   Sunday, Rev. Saulnier

FAYERWEATHER, James   DEAN, Eliza (late J.)   MORE
of Rushville, IL   of Tortuga, W.I. at Christ Ch. 25 Nov. 1834
                         Thurs., Rev. Chaderton

FENWICK, Lewis   FRAY, Catherine   MORE
                         28 Feb., Hyde,JP.   2 March 1842

FERGERSON, Thos. J.   BACON, Elvira M. (Lydele)   MOG
                         at Bonhomme, 18th   22 April 1822

FERGUSON, Wm.   McCARTAN, Mary   MORE
                         Wed., Rev. Davis   4 Oct. 1831

FETTE, H. G.   DAVENPORT, Margaret M.   SCOMB
portrait painter   formerly of Boston   17 June 1835
of St. Louis   14 June, Rev. Drummond

FIELD, David   GWINN, Phebe Ann   MORE
                         16th, Rev. Hinton   20 Jan. 1843

FIELD, J.M.   RIDDLE, Eliza   MORE
both of the Mobile & St. Louis Theatre, at res. C. Keemle 9 Nov. 1837
                         6th, Rev. Potts

FIELD, R. R.   MILLER, Margaretta (late Jacob B.) MORE
                         of Morris Co., NJ   15 March 1845
                         27 Feb., Rev. Vansant
                                                       27

FIELDS, Henry of Boonville.	JACKSON, Adelaide Frances (2nd of Capt. John) of Fauquier Co., VA at Washington, D.C. 24th, Rev. Slicer	COMB 23 Dec. 1847
FIELDS, Jesse	SMITH, Caroline 3rd inst., Rev. N. Childs	SLDU 7 Sept. 1846
FILEKIL, John (Filskil?)	PHILIP, Margaret 1st inst., Philip Cassily, JP	MORE 9 Nov. 1836
FINCH, William M.	GARY, Rachel 20 Sept., Rev. W.H. Lewis	MORE 22 Sept. 1849
FINENTELLE, Charles of Cole Co., IL	MAHEW, Eleanor 17th inst., Kretschmar, JP	SLDU 20 Nov. 1846
FINLEY, Asa	HARVEY, Priscilla 13 Dec., Rev. John Granville	BOWE 9 Jan. 1840
FINNEY, William	LEE, Jane 17 March	MORE 21 March 1825
FISHER, Edward formerly of Jeff. City now merchant at Carthage	SANDERS, Arabella (William) formerly of Indianapolis 18 June	BRUNS 15 July 1848
FITCH, McConal	COOK, Louisa M. 7th inst., Rev. James Cole	OSIN 13 Aug. 1853
FITZWILLIAM, Thomas of Louisiana	WATSON, Eliza (R.D. Esq.) 13th inst., Rev. Donnelly	MORE 15 June 1846
FLEMING, Dr. Robert F. of Philadelphia	LEE, Mary Eliza (Maj. Richard, U.S. Army) 2 June, Bishop Hawks	MORE 4 June 1847
FLEMING, Robert K. late ed. Repub. Advocate	LELAND, Lucina (S.) formerly Worcester, Mass. 11 March, Mr. Hotchkiss (probably at Kaskaskia, IL)	MORE 22 March 1824
FLOOD, John J., Esq. of Linnaeus	MILLS, Mrs. Mary G. formerly of Virginia, in Hinds Co., Miss., the 18th	BRUNS 4 Nov. 1848
FLOURNOY, Hoy of Jackson Co.	HICKMAN, Clarissa (Col. Thos.) of Howard Co. 12 Feb., Rev. Joel Haden	MIN 20 Feb. 1829
FLOYD, David	COCKRELL, Emeline in Franklin last Tues., Bradford Lawless, Esq.	MIN 9 July 1819

FOGLE, Elisha	HARSELL, Harriet 3 April, Rev. Jas. C. Green	PWH 12 April 1849
FOLEY, J.	CHAPMAN, Eliza R. 28th, Rev. Donely	MORE 30 Dec. 1848
FONTAINE, A. M. of Louisville	LASHMUTT, Catherine of Commerce, MO, formerly St.L. 28 Dec. 1843, Rev. Smith	MORE 12 Feb. 1844
FONTAINE, Thomas L.	WATSON, Melinda A. (Robt. G., Esq.) MORE at New Madrid, 25th ult	10 April 1832
FORBES, Leonard of St. Louis	HILLS, Julia Ann at Hartford, Conn. 24 July	MORE 10 Sept. 1836
FORD, Thomas D. of Waterloo, MO	HELM, Matilda T. (Maj. F.T.) at Campbell Co., KY 15 Oct., Rev. Southgate	MORE 22 Oct. 1844
FORREST, William	SLACK, Elizabeth Livingston Co.? 29 Aug., Z. Holcombe, Esq.	MORE 20 Sept. 1850
FORSYTH, Wm. M. of Pittsburgh	HOFFA, Mrs. Catherine of St. Louis 17 May, Rev. Heron, at Pittsburgh	MORE 5 June 1832
FORSYTHE, Robert both of St. Louis County	CULVER, _____ 29th, Rev. Saulnier (BEA 6 Feb. says at Thos. Forsythe's res.)	MORE 2 Feb. 1830
FOSTER, Abial W. of St. Louis	ABRAMS, Ann Eliza formerly of Baltimore, at Andover, IL 24 Sept., Rev. M. Pilsbury	SLDU 1 Oct. 1846
FOSTER, Richard, Esq.	GOOCH, Mary Jane at Shelby Co., 17th	PWH 25 June 1845
FOSTER, Robert	HENRY, Christina at 4th St. Presby. Church 31 May, Rev. John Henning	MORE 9 June 1849
FOSTER, Robert C.	SAUNDERS, Louisa T. (Rev. Turner) SLINQ at Franklin, TN, 28th ult	20 Nov. 1819
FRAZER, John late state of NY	SIMONDS, _____ (N.) at St. Charles, 17th ult.	MOG 17 Aug. 1816
FREELAND, Robert	LEWIS, Elizabeth (late Warner) 3rd, Rev. Chederton	MORE 10 April 1834
FRENCH, Parker of St. Louis	EDWARDS, Lucretia (Hon. Cyrus) of Madison Co. (state not given) 10th	MORE 17 April 1849

FRISTOE, Thomas	JACKSON, Nancy Howard Co. 12th inst, Eb Rodgers	MIN 21 Aug. 1824
FRY, Thomas	HALL, Elizabeth A. 17th, Eb. Rodgers	MIN 29 July 1823
FRYER, James H.	McCULLOUGH, Margaret N. C. Burckhartt	MIN 6 Feb. 1829
FULTON, James	SKINNER, Hannah M. 30 Oct., Rev. Van Court	HORL 6 Nov. 1845
FURGESON, Jonas both of St. Charles	DUGAN, Mary Ann at Barnum's Hotel 29 May, A. Bullard	MORE 31 May 1850
FUSS, Peter of St. Louis	PARCELL, Milvina of and at Burlington, Iowa 21 Nov.	BRUNS 30 Dec. 1848
FULLER, Thomas	KEYS, Mary 1 Jan., J.W. Walsh, JP	MORE 9 Jan. 1838
GAINES, Maj. Gen. E.P. U. S. Army	WHITNEY, Myra Clark (only of late Daniel, Esq. of this city) at Louisiana 17 April, Rev. Clapp	MORE 6 May 1839
GALLAGHER, Bernard of Alton	McLANE, Hannah of St. Louis 23rd, Rev. Tabor	MORE 25 Aug. 1836
GAMBLE, Hamilton R. of St. Louis	COULTER, Caroline J. (late David) at Columbia SC, 8 Nov.	MORE 27 Dec. 1827
GANTT, Thos. T. of St. Louis	TABBS, Mary C. (Moses) at Livingston Co., NY 29 May, Rev. H. B. Bartow	HORL 17 June 1845
GARDNER, A. M. Esq. of St. Louis	PALMER, Eliza C. in Chicago 29th inst., Rev. R. W. Patterson	MOP 6 Aug. 1845
GARESCHE, Alexander of St. Louis	VAN ZANDT, Laura Carnes (eldest of Thomas) in Cincinnati 8th inst., Rev. Driscoll	MORE 11 May 1849
GARESCHE, P. Baudoy, Esq. of St. Louis	McLANE, Juliet (Hon. Louis) in Baltimore 25th ult,	MORE 6 Oct. 1849
GAREY, Henry F. of C of Columbia	BALL, Mary C. of and at New Castle, KY 7th inst., Rev. S. S. Sumner	MORE 14 March 1849

GARLAND, B. S.
of St. Louis

CRESAP, Isabella Jane
late Hampshire Co., VA
in St. Charles Co. at res.
of Wm. T. Sanford
26th, Rev. Patton

MORE
1 May 1838

GARRETT, Frederick
both of Arkansas

RUSSELL, Margaret C.
at res. James Russell, Esq.
Oak Hill, St. Louis Co.
16 April

SWERE
20 April 1846

GARRITY, Dr. James

GANDLEY, Eliza A.
20 Oct., Rev. Fr. Wheeler

MORE
23 Oct. 1850

GATLIN, Major N. C.

SANDFORD, Sciota (Alfred, Esq.)
16 July at Jefferson Barracks
Rev. McCarty

MORE
20 Aug. 1849

GAVIN, William

GRUN, Mary
formerly of Canada
14 Nov., Benj. McKenny

MORE
17 Nov. 1850

GAY, David

LAWRENCE, Eliza H.
formerly Auburn, NY
at Lawrenceville, IL
Sun. last, Rev. Simon

MORE
11 Sept. 1822

GEIGER, Wm. R., Esq.
all of Jefferson Co.

HAVERSTICK, Emilie(Henry, Esq.)
10 March

MORE
14 April 1847

GENSLER, Samuel

MORRIS, L. (only dau. of E.)
24th, Dec. 1845, Rev. S. Samuels
"according to the Mosaic law"

HORL
1 Jan. 1846

GENTRY, Ceato C.

STARR, Emily
1st inst., Rev. C. Parson

SLDU
3 Nov. 1846

GERARD, John B.
of St. Louis

WRIGHT, Letitia
of St. Louis County
28 Jan.

MORE
3 Feb. 1834

GERARD, William
of Ralls Co.

ALLEN, Sarah A.
of Bowling Green, Pike Co.
at res. of Hugh Allen
14 Feb., Rev. Wm. P. Cochran

PWH
22 Feb. 1849

GERARD, William, Jr.

BOYCE, Ann T. (Richard, Esq.)
of Ralls Co.
4 Feb., Rev. W. P. Cochran

PWH
19 Feb. 1845

GERMAN, John

_____(late Thomas B. and Grace) MORE
25 Nov., Fr. Dahman
at St. Francis Xavier

26 Nov. 1850

GEYER, Henry S., Esq.

STARR, Clarissa B.
Thurs., Rev. Giddings

MOG
16 Jan. 1818

GIBBS, Jonathon H.	McFARLAND, Margaret 7th, Rev. Geo. Ekin "published by request"	INP ___ April 1826
GIBSON, Dr. Isaac W. of Spring Hill (Gibson, Wm., p. 34)	TODD, Elizabeth (late Samuel) Livingston Co. 1 Sept., Rev. Wiley Clark	MORE 5 Sept. 1850
GILDERSLEEVE, Noah	JOHNSON, Eliza (Col. J.W.) Thurs., Bishop Rosati	MORE 21 June 1831
GILHULY, Bernard	HIGGINS, Elenor Sun., Rev. Dubourg	MOG 7 June 1820
GLASSCOCK, John	SHEPHERD, Lydia Thurs. last, David Armour	INP 14 Aug. 1821
GLENN, Tyre W. of Louisville	MATTHEWS, Levina of Mississippi in Jefferson Co. 23rd, Rev. Geo. W. Brush	MORE 5 Sept. 1838
GOFORTH, Dr. Wm. G.	HAY, Eulalie (John) at Kaskaskia, 17 April	MOG 3 May 1820
GOLL, Cephas of St. Louis	PARIS, Adeline of and at Louisville 15 Dec., Rev. D. Welburn	MORE 21 Dec. 1844
GOODE, George W., Esq.	WASH, Frances (Judge R.) 16th, Rev. Horrel	MORE 18 July 1846
GOODMAN, Montgomery	NEAL, Mrs. ___ at res. Wm. McPike, Marion Co. 23rd, E. Ballenger	PWH 9 Sept. 1843
GOODRICH, James C.	CHILD, Sarah J. 10 Jan., Rev. H.P.Goodrich	MORE 11 Jan. 1850
GOODWIN, Geo. W.	WADSWORTH, Martha 3 Sept. at Hartford, Conn.	HORL 18 Sept.1845
GOSHEE, Capt. James W. of St. Louis	WHITE, Catherine B. of Jefferson Co. (Ky.?) at res. Frederick Brinkman, Esq. near Middleton, KY 21 Dec. Rev. D. C. Banks	MORE 9 Jan. 1840
GOULD, William Both of St. Louis	COZZENS, Catherine (Chas. W.) at Vicksburg 5 Dec., Rev. Hutchinson	MORE 17 Dec. 1839
GOURD, L. Henry	CHENIE, Rene Marie Julie (late Ante.) of St. Louis 28th, Rev. Pise	HORL 11 June 1846

GRACE, Pierce, Esq.	HARPER, Ann E. (Capt. Andrew) at Lexington, KY 5 Dec., Rev. Stephen Montgomery	MORE 13 Dec. 1844
GRAHAM, Alexander Both of Montgomery Co.	CHANE, Martha 10th, Rev. C. I. Vandeventer	FULT 26 Oct. 1849
GRAHAM, Robert of Grave Creek, VA	FISHBACK, Frances Ann of St. Louis 23rd, Rev. Boyle	MORE 24 July1846
GRAINGER, William	SMITH, Aurelia Clarissa 28 Jan., Rev. C. S. Hawkes	MORE 30 Jan. 1847
GRATIOT, Henry (Charles)	HEMPSTEAD, Susan (Stephen) "some time since"	MOG 6 March 1813
GRATIOT, J.P.B.	PERDREAUVILLE, Marie Antoinette Adele (Rene de David) Thurs., Rev. Dubourg	MOG 24 Nov. 1819
GRATIOT, Paul	BILLON, Virginia	MORE 13 June 1825
GREELY, C. S. of St. Louis	ROBBINS, Emily (late John) of Hartford, Conn. at Brockport, Monroe Co., NY 29 July, Rev. B. B. Stockton	MORE 19 Aug.1840
GREEN, Gen. James	LAVERTY, Sarah Ann formerly Philadelphia 15th, Rev. Boyle, ME Church	MORE 17 Oct. 1842
GREEN, Samuel	WILLIAMS, Sarena (Lewis) 7th, Rev. William Shores	BOLT 23 Jan. 1841
GREEN, William	SMITH, Mrs. Rebecca 20 April, Rev. Perry	MORE 22 April 1843
GREEN, William B.	CARROLL, Mary Sabbath evening, Rev. Van Court	HORL 28 May 1846
GREGG, Leonard	POORMAN, Louisa formerly of Beaver, PA 2nd, Rev. Boyle	HORL 5 Feb. 1846
GREGORY, George H. all of Livingston Co.	GREEN, Julia (or Zulia) Ann 10 Dec. 1848	BRUNS 6 Jan. 1849
GREGORY, Richard A.	MORRIS, Anna at res. Wm. J. Austin 3rd inst., Rev. Tomes	MORE 4 Oct. 1848
GREIG, Wm. both of the U.S. Army (sic)	WALKER, Sarah 7 Sept., S. F. Spalding, Esq.	SWERE 10 Sept. 1848

GIBSON, William	GORDON, Maria 5 January, James Sweney, JP	MORE 8 Jan. 1849
GRENAR, Louis	SCHULTIZE, Christine 27 May, Diogenes Wetmore	SWERE 1847?
GRIMSLEY, Thornton	STARK, Susan Wed., Rev. James E. Welch	SLINQ 19 Aug. 1826
GRINSTEAD, Nathan	WYMER, Elizabeth Tues., Rev. Tabor	BEA 12 April 1832
GUEST, Jonathon Merchant	GANTT, Mary (Dr. E. S.) 8th,	MOG 17 Feb. 1819
GUY, Maj. John R.	MILLER, Elenor A.(late Rev. John) formerly of Newport, Del. 9 March, Rev. Giddings	MOG 23 April 1823
HALDERMAN, Dr. John of Howard Co.	ROGERS, Susannah at Fayette Co., KY 23rd Dec. 1828	MIN 20 Feb. 1829
HALL, John	MUNRO, Eleanor (Capt. Danl.) Thurs. last, by Storrs	MIN 13 May 1823
HALL, Capt. John	MITCHELL, Caroline 4 Aug., Rev. Morris	MORE 5 Aug. 1850
HALLAM, Alexander of St. Louis	GILLESPIE, Caroline of and at Cincinnati St. Paul's Church 20th (26th?), Rev. Johns of Baltimore	MORE 28 Sept. 1837
HALLAM, Alexander of New Orleans	LEWIS, Mary Ann (Thomas, Esq.) at Lincoln Co. Rev. Heyer	MORE 28 Oct. 1841
HALLET, Moses of Franklin, MO	CROWELL, Eunice at Yarmouth, Mass. 11 Feb., Rev. Timothy Allen	MIN 30 April 1819
HALLEY, Presley W. all Howard Co.	THOMPSON, Eunice A. (late Geo.) 6 April, Dr. C. E. Russell	BOLT 12 April 1845
HALSEY, William	BOLLING, Harriet (Wm.) Ralls Co. 2 July, Rev. Isaac Holt	MOAR 10 July 1835
HAMILTON, Rev. Alexander L.	SEAWELL, Nannie P. at res. Judge Wm. C. Douglass Benton Co. 14th, Rev. Josiah Godbey	OSIN 16 April 1853
HAMMOND, John	ROBERS, Mrs. Rebecca (consort late Col. James) 11th inst., Rev. Burns	MORE 15 June 1849

HANENKAMP, R. P.
of Hanenkamp & Co.
of St. Louis

JONES, Agnes C. (Col. Richard S.)   BRUNS
of Aberdeen, Mississippi   28 Oct. 1848
4th

HANLEY, Francis
of Palmyra

ABEL, Elizabeth   PWH
of West Ely   8 Jan. 1845
29 Dec., Rev. Wm. T. Dickson

HANLEY, M. F.

WALTON, S. (James)   MORE
Thurs. last, Elder T.P. Green   7 Feb. 1839

HANNA, James, Esq.
of Marion City

REYNOLDS, Ann (late James, Esq.)   PWH
of Pittsburgh, at Quincy, IL   28 Oct. 1843
26 Oct., Rev. James J. Marks

HANNA, Robert

OWEN, Mary (Gen. I.P.)   MIN
last evening, Rev. Saml. Davis   27 March 1829

HARBISON, John

SCOTT, Mary   MORE
at house of Capt. Thos. Scott   9 Nov. 1850
7 Nov., ____ Pettigraw

HARDEMAN, John

KNOX, Nancy (George)   MIN
Thurs. last, Rev. Justinian   25 March 1823
                    Williams

HARDIN, Thomas
of Columbia

HESSER, Anastasia (Benj., Esq.)   PWH
in Louisiana, Pike Co.   9 Aug. 1849
31 July, Rev. Holt

HARGADINE, William A.
of St. Louis

McCREERY, Acrata A.   MORE
at Hardinsburg, KY   18 Dec. 1850
9 Dec., Rev. Gardinier

HARLOW, Capt. Samuel S.
of St. Louis

PORTER, Lydia Gould   MORE
of and at Greenville, IA   26 Aug. 1847
21 July

HARLOW, William M.

GUERNSEY, Frances J.   MORE
at Collinsville   16 Dec. 1849
16 Dec., Rev. Darrow

HARRINGTON, Jeremiah

FLEMING, Honora   MOG
27th   30 May 1821

HARRIS, Dr. E. D.
recently of N.C.

SMITH, Martha Frances   LEXP
(ygst. of William)   14 Jan. 1845
1 Jan., Rev. M. E. Paul

HARRIS, W. W.
of Brunswick

FRANCISCO, Mary M.   BRUNS
of and at Boonville   11 Nov. 1848
31 Oct.

HARRISON, B. B.
all of Camden Co.

DODSON, P. C.   MORE
27 Sept.   17 Oct. 1846

HARRISON, Enos H. of Brunswick	CUBBERLY, Mrs. Maria C. at res. John Sigerson, Esq. 7th, Rev. Claybaugh	MORE 21 June 1844
HARRISON, Samuel J. of Hannibal	CASKIE, Nannie J. (John) of Richmond, VA 25 Sept., Rev. Norwood	PWH 23 Oct. 1845
HART, George of St. Louis	POTTER, Sarah E. at New London, Conn. 26 Aug., Rev. Edwards	MORE 21 Sept. 1850
HASTINGS, S. W. of New York	VAIL, Julia Frances (Dr. I.) of St. Louis, at Lockport, NY no date	MORE 19 Nov. 1844
HATCH, Samuel of Pike Co.	HAWSHAW, Matilda formerly of St. Louis at Perry, NY 15 Jan., Rev. A. J. Page	MORE 12 Feb. 1845
HAVEN, Charles H. Esq. of St. Louis	THATCHER, Julia Ann (only dau. Daniel, Esq.) of Bridgeport, Conn. Bishop Hawks at Christ Church	MORE 30 March 1846
HAVEN, Charles H., Esq. of St. Louis	RICHMOND, Laura E. (Gales, Esq.) of and at Tremont, Tazewell Co. IL 24th inst.	MORE 31 July 1848
HAWKS, Geo. M. of Portland, ME	DAVENPORT, Almira A. of St. Louis 4 Jan., Geo. Hawks	SWERE 10 Jan. 1848
HAWTHORN, Jacob of St. Louis	SOUTHGATE, Mary L. (Richard,Esq.) of and at Newport, KY 5th, Rev. Bell	MORE 11 Oct. 1843
HAY, Andrew merchant of St. Louis	MORRISON, Emily (William) at Kaskaskia, IL 1st inst.	MORE 10 June 1828
HAYDEN, Julius of St. Louis	LESLIE, Elizabeth B. (niece of Miron, Esq.) of and at Wells Rivert, VT 31 Aug., Rev. S. Thrall	MORE 6 Oct. 1843
HAYDON, _____	HAYDON, Sarah (father decd.) 17 June, Rev. Haycroft	PWH 19 June 1841
HAYES, Benj., Esq. editor Weekly Fountain	CHAUNCEY, Emily (John, Esq.) of Calhoun Co., IL 15th, St. Xavier Ch., Rev. Gliezal(?)	MORE 17 Nov. 1848

HAYES, Westley P. of Boonville	STIVERS, America of Jefferson Co., KY at City Hotel 9th, Rev. Lynn	MORE 11 Oct. 1844
HAYS, Orin both of Bourbon Co., KY	FISHER, Eliza 4 Nov., Cruess	MORE 28 Dec. 1844
HAYWOOD, William H. of Clark Co.	KEISTER, Mrs. Elizabeth of Lewis Co. 30 March, Rev. Smith McMurry	PWH 8 April 1843
HEADLEY, Rev. J. H. all of St. Francois	BAKER, Artimisa at res. Isaac Baker 12th inst., Rev. Andrew Pease	MORE 31 Oct. 1848
HEARD, William T.	BOON, Ann Eliza of Howard Co. 17 Aug., Rev. Heberlin	MORE 25 Aug. 1843
HEARNE, Franklin P. of St. Louis	HIATT, Kate of and at Woodford Co., KY no date, Rev. Cavanaugh	MORE 8 June 1850
HEATH, Jesse W. late of St. Louis	MARCH, Nancy late of NY state at Putnam Co., IL, 22nd	MORE 5 Aug. 1834
HEATON, Dr. O. R.	BLEDSOE, Emily E. (eldest Moses O.) Thurs. last, Rev. Horrell	BEA 1 Aug. 1829
HEDDY, James	DRAKE, Mary Jane 14th inst., Rev. Boyle, Meth.Ch.	MORE 16 Jan. 1844
HEDENBERG, John of St. Louis	CHALLACOMB, Isabella of and at Alton, IL 25 Dec., Rev. A. T. Norton	MORE 5 Jan. 1850
HEELY, Dr. Thos. all St. Louis County	HADWIN, Mary 3rd, Rev. Francis Niel	MOG 9 Jan. 1822
HEISLEN, Aloys at town of Bremen, St. Louis	GERS, Helena Maria 12 Oct., Wetmore, JP	MORE 16 Oct. 1850
HEMPSTEAD, Charles S.	BARNES, Mrs. Eliza of and at Galena 14th, Rev. Kent	MORE 30 Jan. 1834
HEMPSTEAD, Lewis E.	SMITH, Eliza Saturday, Rev. Giddings	MORE 3 Jan. 1828

HEMPSTEAD, Stephen of Dubuque, W.T.	LACKLAND, Lavinia M. late of Maryland in St. Louis Co. 13th (15?), Mr. Larsh	MORE 19 June 1837
HEMPSTEAD, Wm. of St. Louis	BOUTON, Sarah A. of Somers, NY at Galena, IL 22nd, Rev. Kent	MORE 2 June 1836
HENDERSON, George of St. Louis	GODFREY, Mary (Capt. Benj.) of Monticello, VA, no date	SWERE 1 Dec. 1845
HENDERSON, Joseph merchant of Little Rock	ELLIOTT, Eliza Ann (Benj.) of Washington Co., MO at Little Rock, 14 June	MORE 6 July 1826
HENDRIX, Adam of Howard Co.	MURRAY, Isabella J. at Hampstead, MD 19 Sept., Rev. Jas. H. March	BOLT 2 Nov. 1844
HENRY, Isaac ed. Inquirer, St. Louis	BENNETT, Patience (Wm.) of Illinois 28 Sept. at St. Louis	MIN 7 Oct. 1820
HENRY, Thomas	BRODE, Margaret 14 Dec., McDonald, JP	MORE 16 Dec. 1844
HERN, Solomon S. all of Howard Co.	HANNA, Mary J. 25th inst., Rev. Fielding Wilhoit	MORE 31 Dec. 1842
HERNDON, Dr. James H. of Huntsville	TAYLOR, Maria Louisa (James D. of Cinc. Times) no date	BRUNS 21 April 1848
HERYER, Jacob all of Boonville, MO	SNYDER, Eliza 3rd, Rev. Geo. C. Light	BOLT 14 March 1846
HESSER, F. of Brunswick, MO	EVERHEART, Susanah of Lee Co., IA 29 May	BRUNS 8 June 1848
HESTON, Henry J. of Peoria	GRIFFIN, Deborah H. (Peter) at New York, of St. Louis Thurs., Rev. Henry Chase	MORE 5 Nov. 1836
HIBLER, Ephraim of St. Louis Co.	O-ARK, Eliza at Franklin Co. 23 Dec., Rev. James Clark	MORE 5 Jan. 1850
HICKMAN, Capt. P.A. of U.S. Army	BRITTINGHAM, Sarah M. of Hannibal, MO 18th ult., Rev. Fitzgerald	MORE 6 June 1848

HICKS, B. B.	HARSHAW, Margaret A. formerly of Pittsburg 14th, Rev. Tabor	MORE 16 Jan. 1836
HIDDERN, Noah H.	McCOMLEY, Phebe Ann at res. Mr. Demarest, St.L.County 9th	MORE 11 Dec. 1840
HIGGINS, W.W., MD of Lexington	STERETT, Mary E. at Cumberland, MD 13 Aug., Rev.Dr. Symes	MORE 5 Sept. 1850
HILL, Ames	LAWS, Mrs. Sarah 2nd	MORE 21 Dec. 1830
HILL, D. B.	SEELEY, Hannah St. Louis County, Friday	SLINQ 5 April 1820
HILL, Capt. David B. of St. Louis	WALTER, Ann of and at Baltimore 30 Oct., Rev. Smith	MORE 16 Dec. 1828
HILL, Harvey of Boone Co.	SEARCEY, Altazena of Howard Co., Tues. last	MODE 8 Feb. 1847
HILL, John W. of Farmington	POSTEN, Emiline of Hazel Ridge 17 March, Rev. Rogers	MORE 27 March 1847
HILL, Madison	ELSTON, Eliza Boone Co. 9 Sept., Jesse T. Wood, Esq.	MIN 18 Sept. 1830
HIVER, Abraham both of Jefferson City	POSTALL, Mary A. at Chilcot, AR 1 March by Hon. Isaac Baker	MORE 19 May 1842
HODGKINSON, John of St. Louis	HODGKINSON, Margaret Twp. of Grantham St. Catherine, Upper Canada 8 April, Rev. Baynes	MORE 1 May 1844
HOFFMAN, Frederick	SOFFLIN, Mary 24 March, Hyde,JP	MORE 25 March 1842
HOGAN, John S. C. all of Cooper Co.	AINSLIE, Mrs. Mary 20 March, Rev. Corbyn	COMB 6 April 1848
HOLDEN, Edward, Esq.	GALLISON, Charlotte G. (late Harry) at Marblehead, Mass. 31 March, Rev. Lewis	MORE 24 April 1840
HOLDERNESS, William recently of Boston	BENNETT, Mrs. Margaret Ann (dau. G. RAMEY) 14th, Rev. Boyce	MORE 16 Aug. 1843

HOLLAND, Richard E. all of Chariton	DOAK, Lavinia D. at res. Col. J. M. Bell 21st, Rev. Fulton	BOLT 25 Oct. 1845
HOLLIDAY, Maj. Benjamin	BASYE, Elizabeth (Capt. Alfred) Thursday	MIN 26 Aug. 1823
HOLLIDAY, Dr. Charles H. of Doz Peres	CALHOUN, Harriet A. (Geo.,Esq.) near Vincennes, IN 9 Dec., Rev. J.F. Smith	MORE 12 Dec. 1850
HOLLIDAY, Sgt. John D. both of Jefferson Barracks	MITCHELL, Annette 28th, Rev. C. A. Hedges	MORE 2 Feb. 1844
HOLLINGSHEAD, John S.	DAVIS, Mrs. Jane F. in Quincy 23rd ult, Rev. Earhorst	CAMP 2 Feb. 1849
HOLMAN, Richard	CLARK, Susan 9th inst., Rev. John Bull	MIN 21 Dec. 1827
HOLTZCLAW, Richard	SOUTH, Eliza 28 Oct., Rev. Hurley	PWH 4 Nov. 1847
HOMER, Thomas J. of St. Louis	FISHER, Mary Elizabeth (late Jabez, Esq.) at Boston 22 Feb., Rev. Clark	MORE 9 March 1844
HOMES, Frederick of Boston	McKEE, Mary (Mrs. Margaret) of St. Louis 11th inst., Rev. Homes	MORE 13 Sept. 1848
HONEY, J. W.	BATES, Miss at Herculaneum	MOG 19 April 1817
HONEY, John W. all of Herculaneum	AUSTIN, Mary S. (Horace) at Herculaneum 29th	MOG 4 April 1821
HOOD, G. W. formerly of Boonville	McLANE, E. H. of Weston 20th, Rev. Steel	WEJO 4 Jan. 1845
HOOD, Richard of St. Louis	KYRIE, Jane of and at Alton, IL 1 Oct., Rev. Lynd	MORE 16 Oct. 1847
HOOD, Robert merchant at Franklin	BENNETT, Jessie at Philadelphia 6 Feb.	MIN 25 March 1823
HOOKER, Wm.	SHEVINIL, Jane 4 Sept., Thaddeus Wetmore, JP	SWERE 10 Sept. 1848
HOOPER, Clark	BIGELOW, Mary Tues., Rev. Hatfield	MORE 4 Oct. 1833

HOPKINS, William of St. Louis	HOBBS, Laura W. of and at Cincinnati 16th, Rev. Grozer	MORE 23 July 1842
HOPSON, Winthrop, MD of Fayette	CHAPEL, Mrs. Ella A. at Dubuque 30 Sept.	MORE 22 Oct. 1850
HORINE, M. F. of Harrisonville, IL	DRURY, Mrs. Mary at Herculaneum 14 Oct., Rev. Wm. G. Walker	MOAR 23 Oct. 1835
HORINE, Judge M.W.	HALDEMAN, Margaret 8 May, Rev. Wm. Boyle	MORE 9 May 1848
HORN, Dr. Wm. T. of Lone Jack	BROOKS, Angeline of and at Johnson Co. 22 Jan., Rev. Jno. B. Morrow	LEXP 28 Jan. 1845
HOSKINS, Charles 4th Reg., U.S.Inf.	DEANE, Jennie (eld. John,Esq.') of Potosi, at res. Geo. Morton, Esq. 11 March, Rev. Cicero Hawes	MORE 13 March 1845
HOUX, William	OGLESBY, Malvina in vicinity Boonville 16th, James M. Major	BORE 31 Oct. 1843
HOVEY, Edwin	READ, Clarissa (eld. John) at Orono, ME	MORE 29 Dec. 1829
HOWARD, Thomas A.	WEST, Louisa (Maj. Thomas) in Millerburg, Calhoun Co. IL 18th, J.D. Thompson, Esq.	MORE 2 Oct. 1843
HOYER, Edward merchant	HOLLAND, Sarah E. (Col. John) of Tennessee 4 Oct. 1848	BRUNS 7 Oct. 1848
HOYLE, George formerly Lynchburg, VA	CRITTENDEN, Kate (Joel, Esq.) formerly of Georgetown, DC 19 Oct., Rev. Peake	MORE 21 Oct. 1842
HUDSON, John H. of New York	DOYLE, Lucina Julia Ann (Alexander) 30 April, Rev. Horrell	MORE 5 May 1831
HUDSON, Wayne C.	RODGERS, Emily 17th, I. B. Thomas, JP	MORE 25 July 1844
HUDSPETH, Maj. Abijah	ROBINSON, Joanna (4th dau. Capt. Jeremiah) in Madison Co., MO	MORE 29 Nov. 1829
HUFFAKER, George F. of Clay Co.	LOE, Catherine (Thomas) 19th, Rev. Edw. Turner	MIN 21 Jan. 1823

HUGHES, L. F.

LEWIS, Mary (John)
at Cincinnati
10th, Bishop Purcell

HORL
18 Sept. 1845

HUGHES, Richard C.
formerly of Marion Co.

BOWEN, Susan Amanda
of Howard Co.
24th, David D. Stewart

BOLT
28 Feb. 1846

HULL, William C.

BANKS, Louisa Ann (Rev. Danl.C.)
of this city, at Louisville
15th

MORE
21 April 1834

HUME, Michael

PARKER, Sarah
22nd Oct., Cruess

MORE
28 Dec. 1844

HUMPHREY, David

DUFF, Lucinda
of Lincoln Co.
7th, Matthias Nichols, Esq.

MORE
17 Jan. 1838

HUMPHREY, Thos.

BUFORD, Emily
6th, Rev. Jas. Campbell

BGDB
8 March 1845

HUNE, Edward

GRUTTER, Elizabeth (only dau.
Jacob and Margaret)
28 Mar., Rev. E. Hamer

MORE
8 April 1850

HUNT, Ezra
attorney at St. Charles

PETTIBONE, Mariah (late Rufus)
late of this state, at
Hartford, Conn.
no date, no minister

MORE
15 June 1830

HUNT, John F.

GREEN, Adeliza
(late Mrs. Elizabeth)
6th ult, Rev. J. L. Wilson

MORE
20 Oct. 1832

HUNT, Capt. Philemon

ROBERT, Josephine S.
formerly Lexington, KY
Thurs. last, Rev. Horrell

MORE
25 Sept. 1832

HUNT, Robert

McDONALD, Phebe
at Cottage Farm, St.L. County
30th, Rev. Hinton

MORE
31 March 1843

HUNTER, Charles G., Esq.
"all of this city"

PARKS, Emeline
at Pike Co.
6 Sept., Rev. Fenton

MORE
20 Sept.1850

HURD, Wm. T.
of St. Louis

BOON, Eliza
of Howard Co.
17th, Rev. James Heberling

BOLT
19 Aug. 1843

HURT, P. Y.
all Chariton Co.

HARRALDSON, Eliza Frances (Jas.M.)
Wed. last

BRUNS
2 Dec. 1848

HUTCHINGS, John of Paris, KY	HOLTZMAN, Eliza recently of this city at Georgetown, DC, lately	MOG 29 Nov. 1827
HUTCHINSON, John D.	LEWIS, Elzina late of St. Charles 22 April, Black,JP	MORE 24 April 1840
HUTTER, Capt. G.C. U.S. Army	RISQUE, Harriet J. (Maj. J. of Lynchburg, VA) at res. James Kennerly, Jefferson Barracks Tues. last, Rev. Horrel	MORE 13 July 1830
HYATT, Joseph L.	CASON, Martha E. at res. Mrs. Cason 20 Sept., Rev. William Holmes	MORE 1 Oct. 1849
ILLES, Elijah formerly Howard Co.	BENJAMIN, Malinda M. formerly NY, at Sangamon Co.,IL 18 April	MIN 12 June 1824
INNES, Charles of Fayette (?)	RUSSELL, Mary (late Dr.) of MO., at res. Col. T. Ware Bourbon Co., KY 5th inst.	MORE 22 April 1849
ISAACS, Robert	McLENAHAN, Lucy Ann res. Gerald Robinson, Esq. 16th, Rev. Justinian Williams	WESMO 31 Jan. 1834
JACKSON, John	SPARKS, Charlotte T. 26 Dec., Cruess	MORE 28 Dec. 1844
JACOBSON, F. M., MD	POWERS, Rachel late of Little Rock 14 Feb., A. Wetmore	MORE 16 Feb. 1844
JACOBY, Frederick	HOSTER, Caroline 28th, Cruess, JP	MORE 30 Dec. 1848
JAMES, Levi	BUTTS, Ellen (2nd of Col. John) of Caldwell Co. 12 Feb., Rev. Eli Penny	LEXP 4 March 1845
JAMES, William of St. Louis	ROSS, Mary Ann L. formerly of Cincinnati at Kaskaskia Thurs. last, Rev. Matthews	MORE 7 Dec. 1830
JARRETT, E. M.	AESONAGGLE, Paulina near Herculaneum, Jeff. Co. 31 Dec., John Hammond, JP	MORE 7 Jan. 1843
JARRED, Wm. all of Ralls Co.	BOYCE, Ann (Richard) Rev. Cochran	BGDB 15 April 1845

JENNINGS, N.A.   THOMAS, Caroline (Moses, Esq.)   MORE
of St. Louis   of and at Philadelphia   27 Sept. 1838
                        13 Sept.,,Rev. Tyng

JENNINGS, William   FOSTER, Clarissa   COMB
all Cooper Co.   19 Aug., Rev. Jesse N. Pollard   18 Sept. 1847

JEWETT, Jackson   RICHARDSON, Martha (2nd of Elijah) BOLT
all of Howard Co.   13 April, Rev. W. Duncan   24 April 1841

JOHNS, James   MARTIN, Julia   SCMO
                        Sun., Philip A. Sublett   1 July 1820

JOHNSON, Ambrose   COLLINGWORTH, Martha   MORE
                        19th, McKenny, JP   19 July 1846

JOHNSON, Andrew   CUNNINGHAM, Mrs. Caroline   LEXP
                        2 Jan., L. Duncan   14 Jan. 1845

JOHNSON, G. Edward   CARROLL, Mary C.   MORE
of St. Louis   of and at Chestertown, MD   4 Nov. 1839
                        Rev. Jones

JOHNSON, J. W.   GOODING, Mrs. Lucy   MORE
                        Thurs., Rev. Davis   4 Oct. 1831

JOHNSON, James   BROWN, Harriet   MORE
of Boonville   (late Judge Wm. of Harrison Co.KY) 20 June 1846
                        at Island Grove, Sangamon Co.IL
                        11th inst

JOHNSON, John   MURPHY, Elvira (John)   MODE
all of Saline Co.   2nd inst.   10 May 1847

JOHNSON, Samuel   HERSHEY, Barbara Ann (David)   BOLT
all of Howard Co.   2nd, Rev. Wm. Burton   11 Jan. 1845

JOHNSTON, Edward, Esq. RICHARDS, Elizabeth V.   MORE
of Ft. Madison, Iowa   (eld. late Hugh)   20 April 1849
                        "Wed. eve last at res. Gen.
                        Milburn near city" (?)

JONES, George   BENNETT, Cecile   MORE
of St. Louis   at Griggsville, IL   4 Dec. 1850
                        28 Nov., Rev. Stac(?_

JONES, J.   HOWDESHELL, Miss___   MORE
of Bonhomme Twp.   of and at St. Ferdinand's   26 March 1823
                        no date

JONES, R. P.   PRINCE, Sarah (Orestes)   JINQ
                        28 Feb., Rev. Martin Nolan   2 March 1839

JONES, Russell, Esq.
formerly of Georgia

BROWN, Margaret Ann
(Mrs. Margaret) formerly
of Ashley, Pike Co., MO
at Gonzalez Co., TX 18 Oct.
(see also Capt. Andrew Neill)

MORE
24 Dec. 1844

JONES, Thomas
of St. Charles

REYNOLDS, Julia
of Montgomery Co.
20 July, Rev. James Craig

SCMO
5 Aug. 1820

JONES, Wm. Carey
of New Orleans

BENTON, Eliza Preston Carrington
(eldest, Hon. Thomas H.)
18 March

SWERE
5 April 1847

JOPLING, John

LONDON, Mary Ann
23 July, I. B. Thomas, JP

MORE
25 July 1844

KANE, John
both of St. Louis

HOWARD, Mary
at res. of John S. Thompson
Oxford, OH, no date
Joseph Claybaugh

MORE
3 July 1844

KASSON, John A.

ELIOT, Caroline (W.G., Esq.)
in Washington City
2 May, Rev. Wm. Eliot, Jr.

MORE
12 May 1850

KAVANAUGH, Charles M.
of Mississippi

COOPER, May (Col. Joseph)
of Howard Co.
10 April, Rev. Abbot Hancock

BOLT
12 April 1845

KAYSER, Alexander, Esq.
of St. Louis

MORRISON, Eloise P.
(late Col. Wm. of Kaskaskia)
10 April, Rev. Griswold

SWERE
16 April 1849

KEARNY, Maj. S. W.
U. S. Army

RADFORD, Mary
at res. Gen. Wm. Clark
5th, Rev. Horrel

MORE
7 Sept. 1830

KELLAM, Chas. D.

FOUCHE, Louisa
15th, Rev. Gleizal

MORE
18 Nov. 1848

KELLY, Rev. R. N.
of Chariton Co.

WILLIAMS, Harriet Peerce
of Chariton Co.
27 Jan., Rev. John Bull

MIN
12 Feb. 1831

KELSO, Harrison R.

SANDSBURY, Mary
27 April, Rev. R. S. Reynolds

JINQ
5 May 1838

KENDAL, _____

ROUTSANG, Elizabeth
17 March, min. not given

JEFRE
2 April 1842

KENNEDY, John

TIMON, Eleanor
23rd

MOG
30 May 1821

45

KENNEDY, R. V.
editor Western Missourian

PATTON, Frances Noyle (James)
27th ult, Rev. Kerr

BOLT
21 Jan. 1843

KENNEDY, Robert P.
editor Missouri Common-
wealth

CONSTANT, Julia A. Francis (Thos.)
formerly of Springfield, IL
16 March, at Independence, MO
Rev. T. T. Ashby

MORE
28 March 1850

KENNERLY, James

SAUGRAIN, Eliza (Dr. Anthony)
Tuesday last

MOG
14 June 1817

KENNETT, L. M.
of Selma, MO

BOYCE, Martha Ann (eld. John,Esq.)
at Farmington, MO
11th, Rev. Ladd

MORE
18 Sept. 1832

KERR, Augustus
of St. Louis

JENNINGS, Eugenia Malvina
of and at Philadelphia
28th ult., Rev. Furness

MORE
26 Feb. 1833

KERR, James D., Jr.

RULAND, Eliza (late Gen.)   ,
12th inst., Hutchinson

MORE
14 June 1849

KESSELRING, Adam
of St. Louis

ARRAT, Barbara
of Belleville, IL
20th,Thaddeus Wetmore

MORE
22 April 1849

KETCHUM, Samuel
(name given on 8/2 as David)

MUN, Rachel
Centenary Church, W. H. Lewis

MORE
1 Aug. 1849

KEW, William

RUSSELL, Eliza (James)
late of Maryland, at
New Philadelphia, Scott Co.
13th inst., Rev. Smith

MORE
20 Jan. 1837

KEY, Rev. George T.
both of Callaway Co.

HUMPHRIES, Jane
12 Dec., Rev. Redman

MIN
28 Dec. 1833

KEYTE, James
of Chariton Co.

HIX, Eliza
Tues. last

MIN
1 Oct. 1822

KICK, Charles

LaBARGE, Eliza
27th, Rev. Shoemaker

MORE
30 Jan. 1843

KID, Wm. I.
of St. Louis

VON PFISTER, Elizabeth R.
(late Alexander, Esq.) of NY
24th inst., Rev. Hawks

MORE
26 Oct. 1848

KILPATRICK, Dr. T. J.
of Maura Co., TN

SMITHERS, Mary
of Boonville
at Memphis, 5 June, Rev. Green

MORE
16 June 1847

KINDLER, John

WHITEHEAD, Elizabeth
26 Nov., Cruess

MORE
28 Dec. 1844

KING, George
of St. Louis

THOMAS, Elizabeth A. (Phineas) MOP
formerly Hardy Co., VA   27 Nov. 1843
of Franklin Co., MO at Manchester
19th, Rev. John Browne

KINGSBURY, Lt. James W.
1st Reg., U.S. Inf.

CABANNE, Julia (2nd of John P.) MORE
near St. Louis Tues. last   1 June 1830
Rev. Saulnier

KINGSLAND, George
of firm of Bemis, Kings-
land & Lightner of
St. Louis

FERGUSON, Eliza   MORE
of and at Pittsburgh   22 June 1837
17th inst.

KIRKPATRICK, Wm., Esq.
of St. Louis

CASE, Beulah Ann H.   MORE
of Ashtabula, at Cleveland, OH   30 Sept. 1846
21st Sept.

KIRTLEY, Sinclair, Esq.
attorney

PEEBELS, Mary Ann   MIN
in Franklin   12 Feb. 1830
3 Feb., Justinian Williams

KIVETT, Madison
both of Howard Co.

FLEMMINGS, Eliza   BOLT
21st, Elder Wm. M. Burton   2 Oct. 1841

KNAPP, George

McCARTEN, Eleanor (late Thos.)   BOLT
of Fayette, n.d., Rev. Browning 1 Jan. 1841

KNAUSE, Henry
of Cooper Co.

PEALER, Martha Ann (Judge)   BOLT
of Howard Co.   10 Oct. 1846
6th, Wm. B. Hanna

KNEEDLER, Jacob

BLACKISTON, Martha W.   MOAR
formerly Kent Co., Del.   13 May 1839
1 May, Rev. Ames

KNIGHT, Capt. John A.

HUBERT, Celestia   MORE
16 Feb., Diogenes Wetmore   19 Feb. 1847

KOHN, Marcus
of Naples

RONEY, Sarah Jane   MORE
of Exeter at Exeter   11 May 1846
7th inst., Rev. Wm. Williams

KRITZER, Mr. _____

MARKER, Frances Jane   BRUNS
near Utica, Livingston Co.   20 Jan. 1849
7 Jan.

KURLBAUM, Julius W. J.
native of Bielefell,
Westphalia, now Franklin Co.

MAY, Martha Ann   MORE
formerly Sumner Co., TN   14 Aug. 1849
now St. Louis
Rev. Frank Browley

KUYKENDALL, Jacob
of Hampshire Co., VA

CUNNINGHAM, Francis (James)   MIN
of Boone Co.   16 Sept. 1823
28th, Rev. David Doyle   (ca 1822-4)

LaBEAUME, C. Edmund, Esq. of St. Louis	SHAW, Isidora (late Rev. Henry M.) at Vincennes 1 Sept., Rev. Vaux	MORE 7 Sept. 1847
LACKAY, Hugh of Newport, MO	GILMAN, Prudence of St. Louis Thurs. last, Rev. Lutz	MORE 28 May 1833

LA COSSIT - see De La COSSIT

LACY, Benjamin of St. Louis Co.	HYDE, Sarah C. of Crawford Co. 10th inst., Rev. Redman	MORE 27 March 1846
LADD, James S. of St. Louis	ANTHONY, Henrietta B. of and at Zanesville, Ohio 6th inst.	MORE 18 Aug. 1843
LAFFLIN, Sylvester Hall of Saugeties, NY	STAATS, Anna W. (Isaac W. of Weston, adopted dau. of John H. Weaver of St. Louis) 7 Feb., Bishop Hawk	MORE 9 Feb. 1850
LAGRAVE, Antoine	VALLE, Mary (F.B.) of and at Ste. Genevieve 14 Jan., Rev. F.X. Dahman	MORE 27 Jan. 1834
LAMB, Joseph both of St. Louis County	READ, Elizabeth 25 Nov., Cruess	MORE 28 Dec. 1844
LAMONT, Daniel	WILSON, Margaret Thurs., Rev. Potts	MORE 10 July 1831
LAMPTON, James A. H.	HUNTER, Ella E. late of Virginia 13 Nov., Rev. Lyon	MORE 14 Nov. 1849
L'ANDREVILLE, Andre	LaBEAU, Madame "a few days ago"	MOG 19 Oct. 1816
LANE, Nathaniel T. both of Quincy	LEROY, Helen 5 Nov., Rev. Marks	PWH 15 Nov. 1849
LANGHAM, Elias T.	BLAIR, Eliza at farm of Mr. Gallatin Sun. last	MORE 31 July 1822
LANHAM, Stephen of Bonhomme Twp.	CORDELL, Polly of Creve Coeur	MOG 6 Jan. 1816
LANGTON, Jeremiah, Esq.	RIFFLE, Mary 17 Nov., at St. Patrick's Rev. Wheeler	MORE 21 Nov. 1850
LAWRENCE, Elias D. of Louisville, KY	SANFORD, Orphana (Maj. Alfred) of St. Louis Co. 21 Aug. at Christ Church, Bishop Hawks	MORE 22 Aug. 1849

LAY, James H.   MORRISON, Catherine   MIN
                             20 Nov., Rev. Justinian Williams 25 Nov. 1823

LEA, Isaac   McKAY, Ellen   BGDG
of Auburn   of and in Troy   1 April 1845
                             26 March

LEA, Rev. Thos. D.   THOMPSON, Mrs. Sophia Porter   PWH
of Hannibal, MO   of Perry Co., PA   24 Dec. 1846
                             9 Dec., Rev. Wm. Cochran

LEAK, Wm. S.   SAWYER, Rosanna   SWERE
                             15 March, Rev. Linn   19 March 1849

LEAMAN, G. A.   PITTS, Mary Ann   PWH
of Hannibal   formerly of Gardiner, ME   30 Oct. 1844
                             at St. Louis, Rev. J. Boyle

LEAR, Col. John   WOOD, Martha   PWH
of Marion Co.   late of Simpson Co., KY   30 Oct. 1841
                             21 Oct., Rev. H. H. Hays

LEAR, Zachariah   POOL, Mary (Samuel)   PWH
                             of Monroe Co.   23 March 1844
                             14th, Rev. Mussatt

LEDFORD, Wm. H.   CHAMBERLAIN, Julia F.   MORE
of St. Louis   (ygst. of Timothy of   19 Nov. 1848
                             Jacksonville, IL)
                             16 Nov., Rev. Tuthill

LEE, Elliott   WADDLE, Mrs. Poupon   MORE
                                                              24 Jan. 1825

LEE, John   SKINNER, Sophie (Curtis, Esq.)   MORE
                             of Oakland Place, Gravois, MO   11 Dec. 1840
                             8 Dec., Rev. Jos. Tabor

LEER, Henry P.   GROGAN, Rhoda   PWH
of Palmyra, MO   at Jacksonville, IL   16 Oct. 1844
                             Elder David Henshaw

LEFFINGWELL, Hiram W.   SWAN, Mrs. Susan (John Brooks   MORE
                                 or Bricks)   1 Sept.1850
                             at Columbus, OH
                             18 Aug., Rev. A. Doolittle

LEITENSDORFER, Dr. Eugene   ARREN, Soledad (Santiago)   MORE
                             in Santa Fe, 5 Dec.   19 March 1846

LEMMONS, George   HIGHLAND, Alexy Ann   PWH
                             18 March, Elder J. Atkinson   25 March 1847

LEONARD, Abiel, Esq.   REEVES, Jeannette (Benj. H.)   MIN
                             21 Oct., Rev. Justinian Williams 30 Oct. 1830

LESH, Andrew	BILLENS, Sarah Ann 9th inst. at Prairie Grove Watson, JP	SLDU 16 Sept. 1846
LEVI, Solomon J. of St. Louis	JOHNSON, Matilda (P.L., Esq.) of and at Louisville 16th, Rev. Hasie	MORE 22 Jan. 1840
LEWIS, Joshua all of Cooper Co.	TRAVERSE, Susanna (Frank) 26 Aug., Rev. Proctor	MIN 3 Sept. 1819
LEWIS, Samuel W., Esq.	BATES, Adaline (Elias, Esq.) at Herculaneum, Jefferson Co.	MORE 10 Jan. 1825
LICHTENSTEIN, Solomon H.	DeHAAN, Catherine (late Sam'l.) 3 March, Rev. Hirshfield	SWERE 8 March 1847
LICKLIDER, Solomon Lewis late of Shephardstown VA	EDMONSTON, Angeline late of Montgomery Co. MD near St. Charles 28th, Rev. Edmonson	MORE 4 Jan. 1831
LIGHTNER, Isaac of Independence	VALDES, Carmelita of Chihuahua, Mexico, at res. of J. Magoffin, Esq. 2 July, Rev. R. F. Colbourne	LEXP 15 July 1845
LIGHTNER, L. S.	GODAIR, Elizabeth at res. Daniel Steinbeck n.d., Rev. John C. Harbison	INP ___ Aug. 1823
LILLEY, John	BRADY, Mrs. ____ Thurs. at St. Charles	MORE 11 Sept. 1822
LINDELL, Peter, Jr.	NIMAN, Ellen (Peter, Esq.) of and at Brownsville, PA 29th, Rev. Parmer	MORE 5 Dec. 1848
LINDSAY, Hiram, Esq. of Atlas, IL	LYNCH, Rosina of St. Louis, at Atlas, IL 18th, Rev. Stedman	MORE 27 March 1832
LINDSLEY, J. C. of St. Louis	GIBBS, Abbey F. of and at Boston 19th ult.	MORE 5 Sept. 1838
LINK, John Henry	SPURR, Susan 6th, I. B. Thompson, JP	MORE 10 Oct. 1843
LITTLE, John	LABADIE, Mrs. Marie Antoinette no date	MOG 19 Oct. 1816
LITTLETON, Capt. M. of St. Louis	TOWER, Mary L. of Elizabethtown, at Pittsburgh Rev. Eaton	PWH 15 July 1843

LIXON, Elias	LAFLIN, Mary Ann Spalding, JP	MORE 31 July 1850
LLOYD, James F. of Louisville	DePREFONTAINE, Mary Ann (James) 1 April, Rev. W. W. Kitzmiller	MORE 3 April 1850
LOCKWOOD, Judge J.H. of Prairie du Chien, IL	WRIGHT, Sarah Ann at Major Wrights' near St. Louis 5th inst., Rev. Chederton	MORE 13 March 1834
LOCKWOOD, Hon. Saml. Drake	NASH, Mary Virginia Stith at res. Col. Francis Nash in St. Louis Co. 3rd inst.	MORE 12 Oct. 1826
LOKER, C. R.	WRIGHT, Mary Jane 11th, John W. Colvin, Esq.	MORE 13 Dec. 1844
LOKER, Wm. M. of St. Louis	LOKER, Anna (Wm. H., Esq.) of St. Mary's Co., MD at St. Mary's Church, 18th ult	MORE 1 Aug. 1848
LONG, John F.	PIPKIN, Frances E. at Gravois 29th, Thos. Sappington	MORE 3 Oct. 1836
LONGACRE, John	LONGACRE, Isabella in Jefferson Co., 10th inst.	MORE 26 Feb. 1846
LONGMIRE, William	BOURN, Mrs. Christian Tues. last, Rev. Young	PWH 16 March 1844
LORIMIER, P. A. of Michigan Territory	HEMPSTEAD, Mary L.(Stephen, Jr.) of St. Charles 6th inst., Rev. Smith	MORE 11 May 1830
LOWE, John	SLATER, Carolina 7 March, Rev. Tucker	SWERE 15 March 1847
LOWRY, E. P., M.D. all of St. Charles	BOONE, Jane A. (late J.W., Esq.) 4th inst., Elder J. Patton	MORE 6 Jan. 1848
LOWRY, Dr. Wm. F. (Dr. J. J.) all Howard Co.	YATES, Georgia Ellen (George, Esq.,) 2nd	BRUNS 24 Feb. 1848
LUCAS, B. F. of Carroll Co.	WOLFSKILL, Elizabeth of Livingston Co. 25th	BRUNS 4 Nov. 1848
LUKE, J. W. of St. Louis	WILSON, Catherine W. of Dubuque, Iowa at Dubuque 10 Nov., Rev. J. Depui	MORE 22 Nov. 1847
LUNDY, P. F.	OLDRUM, Elizabeth in Callaway Co., the 16th	MORE 6 Dec. 1847

LYMAN, James of St. Louis	DICKINSON, Frances R. of and at Northampton (?) 6 Sept., Rev. Wiley	MORE 8 Oct. 1838
LYNN, Wm. of Ste. Genevieve	DUNCAN, Miss_____ of Cape Girardeau Thursday	SLINQ 8 Dec. 1819
LYONS, _____	JOHNSON, Eliza 2 Jan., L. Duncan	LEXP 14 Jan. 1845
McARDLE, James of St. Louis	DAVIS, Nancy of Pittsburg	SWERE 15 Dec. 1845
McBRIDE, A. S.	MADDOX, J. B. 17th inst., Capers	MORE 31 May 1848
McBRIDE, F. C., Esq. formerly of Philadelphia	O'FALLON, Mrs. Sophia of Jefferson Co. 13 Jan.	MORE 31 Jan. 1848
McCAMPBELL, Thomas C.	GOWDY, Anna (Thos., Esq.) of St. Louis, at Nashville 20th inst., Rev. Edgar	MORE 28 Oct. 1846
McCAUSLAND, David	HEALD, Mary S. of St. Charles Co. 10th, Rev. Bainbridge	MORE 16 Oct. 1832
McCLELLAND, James Bruce, Esq. of Nelson (VA?)	OTEY, Nannie L. (Dr. W.L.) formerly of Bedford Co. VA at res. E. Logwood, Esq., in VA 26 Feb., Rev. E. J. Newlin	MORE 23 March 1850
McCLURE, Samuel	PATTON, Elizabeth 30th, Rev. D. Shumate	HORL 14 May 1846
McCOLLOUGH, Andrew	GODMAN, Nancy (Granny S.) near Huston 20 Dec.	PWH 24 Feb. 1844
McCLURE, Capt. Wm.	SLAVENS, Elizabeth (Wm. Esq.) 27 March, Rev. A. Woods	MIN 29 March 1834
McCORD, John all of Platte Co.	MILLER, Sarah 13 Feb., Rev. Thos. Turner	SALT 7 March 1840
McCREERY, Phocion R. of St. Louis	HAYNES (HYNES?), Mary Jane (Col. Andrew) of and in Nashville 8th inst.	MORE 15 Oct. 1846
McCUNE, John S. of Louisiana, Pike Co.	GLASBY, Ruth Anna, formerly Chester Co., PA at res. of brother A.H. Glasby, Clinton Mills 21st, Rev. Campbell	MORE 27 May 1839

McCURDY, Fleming B. of Boonville	MARSHALL, Nancy of and at Pinckney, Warren Co. 4th inst., Rev. James McBride	MORE 12 Dec. 1834
McDONOUGH, Augustus Rodney of St. Louis	McVICKER, Frances Brenton at Utica, NY 10th, Rev. Geo. Leeds	HORL 25 June 1846
McDONALD, John W.	PASQUIER, Virginia Pelagie	SWERE 2 March 1846
McENNIS, Michael	DUNN, Eliza at St. Patrick's Church 12th inst., Rev. Wheeler	MORE 13 Feb. 1849
McFADIN, James M. of Lexington, MO	TRIPLETT, Ann Todd of Georgetown 19th, Rev. Linn	MORE 22 Sept. 1844
McFARLAND, John	HOUX, Elizabeth (Frederick) in Cooper Co. 7th inst., Justinian Williams	MIN 14 Oct. 1823
McGARY, James D.	MURRY, Nancy A. (Enoch) of Round Prairie, Callaway Co. in Columbia, n.d.	MIN 10 Jan. 1835
McGEE, Hugh all of Wayne Co.	TARLTON, Jane (Gen.) 22 May, James Wilson	INP ___ May 1825
McGILL, Theodore	TISON, Adele (Albert) "near this place" Sat., Rev. Niel	MORE 13 Aug. 1823
McGIRK, Andrew S. of Franklin	PARRISH, Elizabeth J. of and at Montgomery Co. 17th inst.	MIN 29 Jan. 1822
McGREADY, Wm. Edward	DUNKLIN, Eliza Lucinda (Stephen T., Esq.) 28th, Rev. Andrew Pence	MORE 1 Jan. 1844
McGUIRE, John	BURNS, Mary Ann 25th, Bishop Kemper	MORE 27 Feb. 1839
McILVAINE, Joseph	HILLS, Harriet Rosetta 18 Feb., Rev. Weed	SWERE 22 Feb. 1847
McKAY, Harrison B. of St. Louis	JENNINGS, Sarah Maria (late Rev. Obadiah) of Nashville, TN at Philadelphia 10 Feb., Rev. Boardman	MORE 23 Feb. 1842
McKee, Hiram of St. Louis	TRUESDALL, Nancy of Franklin Co. 21st, Rev. James N. Rule	MORE 31 May 1833

McKEE, Isaac H.   PAUL, Mary Ann (Hugh)   MORE
                                                                      23 June 1847

McKENZIE, Roderick Charles   McKEE, Mrs. Bridget Martha Roy   MORE
                                    at St. Joseph   2 Sept. 1850
                                    15 Aug., Rev. Thomas Scanlan

McKENZIE, Wallace   HAMILTON, Mary   MORE
                                    9 June, Alphonso Wetmore   5 June 1846

McKINNEY, Samuel T.   WOOD, Rachel J.   MORE
                                    6 Oct., Rev. R. Maudesley   8 Oct. 1849

McKINSEY, James   NICHOL, Catherine   MORE
                                    at res. John Balcour   6 Jan. 1844
                                    1 Jan., Rev. Griswold

McKNIGHT, Thomas   SCOTT, Fanny (sister of John)   MOG
                                    at Ste. Genevieve   19 Nov. 1814

McLARD, Capt. James   SHAW, Mary .   SLAM
of steamboat Gov. Briggs   of St. Louis   3 March 1845
                                    9th inst., Rev. Lumsden

McLAUGHLIN, John   DE LA TOUR, Julia A.   MORE
                                    late of Philadelphia   5 Feb. 1849
                                    30 Jan., Rev. Appleton

McLURKEN, Thomas   SLADE, Mrs. Eloise   MORE
of St. Louis   (dau. of Sidney BREEDS)   10 Aug. 1850
                                    at Carlyle, IL 8 Aug.

McMANUS, William   SIMMONS, Cammelio   MORE
of St. Louis   of and at Pittsburgh   10 Jan. 1844
                                    28th ult., Rev. Bryant

McMULLEN, Oliver H.   MELLOR, Jane E. (James, Esq.)   MORE
                                    of and at Wheeling, VA   8 Feb. 1847
                                    28 Jan., by pastor of
                                    New Jerusalem Church

McNAIR, A. R.   McCLAREY, Mary Magdalena   MOAR
of St. Louis   at New Orleans   12 June 1835
                                    15 April, Rev. Mullen

McNUTT, Samuel   McBETH, Catherine A.   SWERE
                                    2 July   6 July, 1846

McPAUL, Charles   JUDIE, Leonora A. (eldest, Joseph) MORE
of St. Louis   at Baltimore   22 Oct. 1850
                                    10 Oct., Rev. A. J. Elder

McPHEETERS, Dr. Wm.   SELDEN, Pink(ygst. late Cary)   MORE
                                    of Washington City, at Montrose   13 June 1846
                                    nr. St. Louis, 11th inst., Bishop Hawks

McQUEEN, J. P. Dudley of Pike Co.	SANFORD, Nancy of Lincoln Co., near Auburn Wed. last, Rev. J.W. Campbell	BGDB 1 April 1845
McREYNOLDS, Allen of Saline Co.	COOPER, Amanda of Lafayette Co. 15th, Benj. Y. Yantis	WEM 23 Jan. 1840
MACRAE, N. C. U. S. Army	CLARK, Gwinthlean (niece of Maj. J. Green, U.S.Army) at Ft. Armstrong, Rock Island,IL 1st, Rev. A. W. Casad	MORE 16 Sept. 1828
MAFFITT, William	CHOUTEAU, Julia (P., Jr., Esq.) in New York 1st inst., Rev. Powers	MORE 14 June 1843
MAGENIS, A. L. of St. Louis	McREA, Mary (Col.___,U.S.A.Art.) in New York, 22nd	MORE 8 Nov. 1831
MALONE, Calvin of steamboat Pawnee	SMITH, Julia of Cape Girardeau 23rd ult., Rev. Brandis	MORE 30 May 1839
MALONE, Capt. Richard all of Chariton	MEDLEY, Eliza (Jacob) 9th inst., Rev. Saml. Davis	MIN 14 Dec. 1827
MANN, Alfred	RENNICK, Ann 7th, Rev. Lutz	BEA 16 Feb. 1832
MANNING, B. F. of New Orleans	PAGE, Susan of St. Louis 26th, Rev. B. F. Braddock	MORE 28 Sept. 1837
MANNING, John F. all of Chillicothe, MO	SCOLEY, Eveline B. (Dr.E.D.) 27 Aug., Z. Holcombe, Esq.	MORE 20 Sept. 1850
MANNING, Michael	FULBACK, Mrs. Rosanna 19 Sept., Bishop Hawks	MORE 21 Sept. 1850
MANTIAL, Castara	MORIN, Natalie 29th, D. Wetmore	MORE 31 July 1844
MANTZ, Charles A.	WINDSOR, Caroline 26th inst., E. J. Palmer	MORE 29 April 1849
MARCH, Col. E. C. of St. Louis	UNDERHILL, Augusta Antoinette (A.L.) of and at New York City 29th ult.	MORE 27 Nov. 1832
MARSH, Darius	HARDY, Sarah Ann 20 Oct., Rev. Minard	MORE 11 Nov. 1841
MARSHALL, L. P. both of Franklin, Mo.	KNOX, Sarah 3 Sept., Rev. H. Chamberlin	MIN 18 Sept. 1829

MARTIEN, Dr. James M.   CALWAY, Frances E.   MORE
                               (Joseph P. and Nancy)   9 July 1847
                               of Callaway Co.
                               3 July, Wm. J. Gilman, Esq.

MARTIN, James   ALBRIGHT, Catharine   MOG
from Ohio   of St. Louis   24 March 1819
                               15th, Rev. James E. Walsh

MARTIN, John M.   FALWELL, Elizabeth Ann   COMB
                               of Louisville, KY   29 July 1835
                               aboard steamboat Rapide
                               en route Louisv.-St. Louis
                               26 July, S. H. Kimmel, Esq.

MARVIN, Enoch M.   CLARK, Harriet B.   HORL
                               23rd, Rev. Jno Hogan   25 Sept. 1845

MASON, Luther, Esq.   PRICE, Martha M.   MORE
of Missouri   of Nicholasville, at Lexington,KY 29 Sept. 1841
                               21 April, Rev. J. P. Coons

MASSEY, Benj. F.   WITHERS, Maria   WEM
of Barry Co.   of Cooper Co.   13 June 1839
                               11th, Rev. F. F. Peake

MATHEWS, Rev. John   SMITH, Ann   MOG
of Louisiana   of and at Bonhomme   10 May 1820
                               4th, Rev. Charles S. Robinson

MATTHEWS, James P.   COGSWELL, Fanny (Col. Wm.)   MORE
                               "at Cogswell's Landing"   7 June 1850
                               28 May(?), Rev. Symmington

MATTHEWS, John   BARNES, Susan H.   JINQ
of Jefferson City   of Henry Co.   11 April 1844
                               25th, Rev. Chandler

MATTHEWS, John S.   HOLDING, Mary Elizabeth   MORE
of St. Louis   of and at Salisbury, Del.   3 Nov. 1840
                               15 Oct., Rev. Jefferson

MACUBIN, Charles N., Esq.   FAY, Ellen Maria (late Nahum)   MORE
of Chicago   12th Congreg. Ch., Boston   29 June 1846
                               17th inst.

MADISON, James   HAYDEN, Evaline   PWH
                               last Thurs., Rev. Atkinson   14 Oct. 1847

MATTOX, Thos.   DRAGOON, Temperance   MORE
both of Lebanon, IL   27th inst., McKenney, JP   28 Sept. 1837

MAURICE, W. H.   ANDREWS, Sarah F.   MORE
of St. Louis   of Boston, in Louisville   8 Nov. 1848
                               6th inst., Rev. Jno. Haywood

56

MAWDESLEY, Richard	DANIELS, Catherine 23rd, Rev. J. Mackoy	HORL 26 Feb. 1846
MAXFIELD, E. C.	OWENS, Jane of St. Clair Co., IL 13 Dec., Cruess	MORE 28 Dec. 1844
MAXWELL, Henry of St. Louis	DAVID, Caroline B. (Jacob) of and at Philadelphia 15 Aug., Rev. G. C. Cuyler	MORE 31 Aug. 1839
MAXWELL, Henry	CUMMINGS, Martha A. (James) 26 Sept., Rev. Boyle	MORE 1 Oct. 1844
MAXWELL, James G.	REILLY, Ann M. late of Baltimore 2 Feb., Rev. J. Boyle	MORE 4 Feb. 1845
MAXWELL, Capt. Thomas	SHERMAN, Lucinda (eld. David) at Hickory Grove, Montgomery Co. 4th ult, Rev. Geo. Clay	MORE 17 May 1831
MAYO, Peyton Randolph, MD of Cooper Co.	PRENTIS, Mrs.Caroline Cornelia of Frankfort, at res. Col. John Vickers, Muehlenberg Co.KY Rev. Kincheloe	MORE 4 Dec. 1850
MEADE, Dr. D. E.	WEEKS, Harriet C. (late David of Attakapas, LA) 3 Nov.	SWERE 30 Nov. 1846
MEGAFFIGAN, Peter of New Orleans	GILBRETH, Jane C. of St. Louis 14th, Rev. Patton	MORE 17 Dec. 1841
MELODY, George H.C.	GAW, Jane at Franklin 29th, Rev. Justinian Williams	MORE 14 Oct. 1829
MERRITT, J. D. of New York	WARD, Georane E. (John) of Lincoln Co. 21st inst., Rev. Bainbridge	MORE 31 May 1833
METCALFE, Wm.	O'HARA, Margaret Thurs. last, Rev. Tabor	MORE 17 June 1837
MILAM, James V.	MASSEI, Judith Ann (sic, prob. Massie) 25 Oct., Rev. Cochran	PWH 31 Oct. 1840
MILAN, J. C. one of props. of "Sentinel:	BARNETT, Mary E. (Rev. W.B.) of Prairieville, Pike Co. 7th inst., Rev. J.C. Berryman	GLWT 21 Oct. 1852

MILBURN, William
both of St. Louis

RICHARDS, Mrs. Mary V.
at res. Dr. Somes, Vincennes
7 Oct., Rev. Kilkelly, Episcopal

MORE
19 Oct. 1839

MILES, Edmund

WELLS, Emely Elenor
late of Wheeling
6 Sept., Rev. Minard

MORE
10 Sept. 1841

MILLEGES, Richard

GUYON, Mlle. Felicite
Monday

MORE
27 Nov. 1822

MILLER, George W., Esq.
all of Jefferson City

BASEY, Louisa (Maj. Alfred)
Rev. W. P. Cochran

MIN
5 May 1832

MILLER, P. J.
one of editors St.L.Times

HACKNEY, Ariadne (Aaron)
of and at Mercer, PA
30 Aug., Rev. Dinwiddie

MORE
20 Sept. 1831

MILLER, Wm., Esq.

WASHINGTON, Mary
25 April, A. Wetmore

MORE
27 April 1844

MILLER, Wm. H.

WOODSON, Paulina
in Monroe Co.
"Sun. last", Isaac Coppedge, Esq.

BGBD
8 Feb. 1845

MILLS, R. B.
of steamboat Oceana

PIERCE, Lucy M. (Col.)
at Boonville
6th, Rev. T. Johnson

BOLT
10 June 1843

MING, James M., Esq.
of Port. Wm. (MO? MD?)

OSBORNE, Jemima (Wm., Esq.)
in Franklin Co.
28 Oct.

MORE
12 Nov. 1846

MITCHELL, Edward
of Springfield, IL

ESSEX, Eleanor
of St. Louis
Thurs., Rev. Corson

MORE
15 Nov. 1831

MITCHELL, Leonard

BURK, Mary Ann
13 Aug., Rev. Patterson

MORE
18 Aug. 1840

MITTELBERGER, John C.

MALLERSON, _____ (Elijah)
at St. Charles
23 Dec., Rev. Fielding

MORE
1 Jan. 1842

MONROE, John T.
of Linn Co.

SHEPHERD, Rebecca Isadora
(late Capt. William)
at New Orleans
11th, Rev. W. H. Watkins

HORL
9 Oct. 1845

MONTAGUE, Joseph

TAYLOR, Mary Jane
12 July, Rev. N. Childs

MORE
13 July 1850

MONTAIGNE, Joseph, Jr.

GUITARD, Julia (widow of Vincent)
11 March, Shepard, J.P.

MORE
17 March 1840

MONTGOMERY, Thomas J.

NOYES (Noyce), Sarah C.
(John P.)
30 Nov., Rev. Dr. Goodrich

SWERE
6 Dec. 1847

MOORE, Daniel Sharp Delany

PARMER, Ann (Col. Martin)
at Bluffton, Ray Co.
7 March, Wm. P. Thompson, JP

MIN
12 April 1825

MOORE, G. W.
of St. Louis

LACY, Lydia
at Prairie du Long, IL
Squire Sowers

MORE
26 July 1849

MOORE, George W.
of St. Louis

McCORMICK, C. C.
of Rutland, VT, at San Francisco
22 Oct.

MORE
16 Dec. 1850

MOORE, Jonas, Esq.

ROBBINS, Savinia N.
of Jefferson Co., NY
1 May, Rev. Joseph Tabor

MORE
3 May 1839

MOORE, William

WOLF, Anna Catherine
24 Sept., Samuel Hanson

JINQ
26 Sept. 1844

MORAN, Francis

COOK, Susan
25 Dec., Cruess

MORE
7 Jan. 1843

MOREHOUSE, Capt. Legrand

LOOMIS, Julia M.
at Christ Church
4 Sept., Bishop Hawks

MORE
6 Sept. 1849

MORGAN, Henry
of St. Louis

YEATMAN, Elizabeth (Henry L.of VA)
at Cincinnati
27 April, Rev. Brook

MORE
2 May 1843

MORELAND, Capt. Daniel
formerly Rhode Island

HAYES, Griselda
late Ontario Co., NY
4th, Rev. Robinson

SCMO
11 July 1821

MORRIS, S. A. Esq.
of Howard Co.

BATES, Ann Eliza
of Batesville, Albemarle Co. VA
18 Oct., Rev. Wm. W. Jones

MORE
6 Nov. 1849

MORRISON, William V.
of St. Louis

COLEMAN, Mary Ann
of and at Harrison Co., KY
21 March, Rev. Ganno

MORE
1 April 1839

MOTT, John H.
of St. Louis

VANDENBURGH, Jane Ann (James,Esq.)
of and at New York
11th, St. Luke's Ch., Rev. Forbes

MORE
23 Aug. 1842

MUIR, Wm., E., Esq.
of Louisiana

ARMSTRONG, Eliza (Col. Robert)
Thurs., Rev. Potts

MORE
6 Sept. 1831

MUIRFELDT, H. W. of St. Louis	WARDEN, Mary Frances of and in New York 29th, Rev. E. Tucker	MORE 12 March 1844
MULFORD, Charles	PARVIN, Elizabeth of Galena, IL 31 Dec., Rev. Weed	SWERE 3 Jan. 1847
MULLEN, T.	DUNN, Mary A. 20 Aug., Rev. Wheeler	MORE 31 Aug. 1850
MUNN, Ira Y.	SCOTT, Mary (only dau. James) 25th, Rev. Tabor	MORE 28 Dec. 1839
MUNSON, Rev. A.	KING, Serena A. of Washington, Franklin Co. 1 March, Rev. Gilbreath	MORE 4 March 1842
MURDOCK, Francis B. of Alton, IL	JOHNSON, Mary (Col. John) yesterday, Rev. Lutz	MORE 9 May 1838
MURRAY, John G. late of Philadelphia	WARRANCE, Priscilla H. Wed., Rev. Tabor	MORE 5 Nov. 1836
MURRAY, Joseph	BRUMBAUGH, Mary 18th, Hyde, JP	MORE 19 Aug. 1844
MURRELL, Jos. P. of Lynchburg, VA	RICKMAN, Mary of and at St. Louis 16th, Rev. J. H. Linn	MORE 20 Jan. 1848
NALLEY, Alexander of Carondelet, St. L. Co.	SEVAYES, Mrs. Carmel of Santa Fe 18 Oct.	MORE 1 Jan. 1846
NASH, Gilbert of St. Louis	HARBORD, Eliza C. of and at Philadelphia St. Phillips Church 31 Dec., Rev. Neville	MORE 15 Jan. 1848
NEGUS, Isaac, Jr. of Green Co. (IL?)	REED, Maria (Isaac S.) of St. Clair Co., IL 6th, Rev. Nolin	MORE 18 Sept. 1832
NEIL, Robert	WARE, Sarah E. 12th, Rev. Homes	HORL 16 April 1846
NEILL, Capt. Andrew attorney (see also Jones, Russell)	BROWN, Nancy Agnes (late Dr. Hugh H.) formerly Pike Co., MO at Gonzalez Co. TX 18 Oct.	MORE 24 Dec. 1844
NEILL, Joseph of Kentucky	KINKAID, E. of and at Creve Coeur, St.L.Co. Thurs., T. Mason	MORE 22 March 1820

NELSON, Dr. Arthur | GANTT, Elenora | MOG
 | 25th ult, Rev. Edward Gantt | 2 June 1819

NELSON, Thomas | PETERSON, Margaret | MORE
 | Thurs. last, Rev. Horrell | 14 July 1829

NELSON, Capt. Wm. S. | CASE, Catherine (John, Esq.) | MORE
of St. Louis | of and at Utica, NY | 16 Oct. 1846
 | 29 Sept.

NEWMARK, A. | LEVY, Jane (Michael) | HORL
 | of NY City, 3rd inst | 4 Dec. 1845
 | Jos. Newmark, Esq. "according
 | to the Mosaic law"

NEWTON, Thomas W. | CORDELL, Amelia C. (E.B. of | MORE
of Little Rock, AR | Jefferson City) at res. | 28 Feb. and
 | Col. J. H. Llewellyn, | 13 March 1850
 | Chicot Co., AR
 | 14 Feb., Bishop Freeman

NICHOLS, Arthur | YOUNG, Catherine (ygst. late | MORE
of St. Louis | Ezra of South-east NY) | 6 Nov. 1849
 | 26 Oct., NY

NORRIS, James | GEYER, Harriet (Henry, Esq.) | MORE
 | 19th, Bishop Hawks | 20 May 1846

NOWLIN, Peyton, Jr. | PULLIAM, Martha M. (Drury) | MIN
 | of Saline Co., 28th | 2 Nov. 1827

OBUCHON, Francis | CALLOT, Judith (widow Deguire) | SOV
 | 6 Feb. 1833 | 9 March 1833

O'FALLON, Maj. Benj. | LEE, Sophia (Patrick) | MORE
of U.S. Ind. Dept. | of St. Charles, Judge Pettibone | 12 Nov. 1823
 | n.d.

OLIVER, Obediah | LEPARD, Elizabeth | FULT
 | 5th, Rev. Noah Flood | 15 Dec. 1848

ORR, Major Wm. | FOULKE, Minerva (eld. Philip) | MORE
one of editors of | at Kaskaskia | 31 May 1827
St. L. Commercial Advertiser

ORTON, Oliver | HOY, Sarah D. | BRUNS
all of Livingston Co. | 7 Jan. | 20 Jan. 1849

OSBORN, William H. | SHEAFE, Auguste Haven (Jacob, Esq.) MORE
of New Orleans | of Pottsville, PA, in Louisiana, 23 April 1847
 | Pike Co., MO 21 April
 | Rev. Griswold

61

OSBURN, Nicholas C.	RICHARDS, Sidney 29th, Rev. Horrell	HORL 5 Feb. 1846
OSBORNE, John J. of New Orleans	STANLEY, Frances Ann (2nd dau. of Samuel of St. Louis) at New Orleans, Rev. Koehner	MORE 15 July 1849
OTIS, Benj. F.	SWAIN, Sarah E. of Worcester, MA 21 Aug.	MORE 8 Sept. 1848
OUDARD, Louis, P.A.	BENSVILLE, Mme. Celine D. 18 Oct.	SWERE 20 Oct. 1845
OWENS, Elias	THOMPSON, Christine Nancy (R.W., Esq.) 2nd, Rev. Paris	MORE 4 July 1848
OWENS, Stephen B.	PORTER, Mary Ellen 13th, McKinney, JP	HORL 26 June 1845
PACKARD, Bryant A.	LOCKE, Mary 16th, Rev. Holmes	HORL 23 Oct. 1845
PAGE, Francis W. of St. Louis	STODDARD, Jane M. of and at Allenton, AL at res. of Mayor, C.H. Swift 26 April	MORE 11 May 1842
PAGE, William of Alton, IL	DOUGLASS, Eliza of St. Louis 13th inst., Rev. C. A. Farley	MORE 16 May 1838
PAPIN, Hypolite	LOISEL, Josephine 4th, Rev. Francis Savine	MOG 8 July 1815
PAPIN, Silvestre	SCOFIELD, Emeline at Clinton, Michigan 17th, Rev. Genton	MORE 28 Jan. 1850
PARKER, Edward	RUSSELL, Mrs. R. 30 Sept., Benj. McKinney	MORE 13 Oct. 1850
PARKER, Henry S. of St. Louis	HAMILTON, Jane (John G.) of and at Monticello, IL 28th inst., Rev. Chamberlain	MORE 31 Aug. 1848
PARMER, Anthony C. Sheriff of St. Charles	AYRES, Rebeckah A. (Ebenezer) at St. Charles, n.d. Rev. Flint	MOG 10 Feb. 1819
PASCHALL, N. one of eds. MORE	EDGAR, Mrs. M. Eliza of Kaskaskia, at Springfield,IL 27th ult., Rev. Bergen	MORE 4 Dec. 1832
PATTERSON, David	WINN, Rebecca Boone County 2 Jan., Jesse Wood, Esq.	MIN 25 Jan. 1828

PATTERSON, Joseph Collector of Howard Co.	BURKE, Elizabeth W. 11th, Rev. Bull	MIN 23 Oct. 1821
PATTERSON, N.	HIGGINS, Winifred (Wm.) Saturday, Rev. Saulnier	MORE 1 Nov. 1827
PATTON, John W. H. Printer	RUBEY, Elizabeth A. (Henry) 13th	MODE 5 Jan. 1848
PATTEN, Nathaniel Editor Mo. Intelligencer	GAITHER, Matilda 3rd, Rev. Augustus Pomeroy at Fayette, Howard Co.	MORE 21 June 1827
PATTEN, Col. Thomas W.	GIVENS, Sarah F. Howard Co., n.d., Joseph Sears	MIN 15 Jan. 1824
PATTON, Nathaniel Editor Mo. Intelligencer	HOLMAN, Mrs. Eliza Ann (late Col. Saml. Williams) at town of Chariton, 27th ult.	MORE 8 March 1831
PAUL, Dr.	CHOUTEAU, Miss __ (Auguste) at parish church a few days ago	MOG 25 April 1812
PAUL, Gabriel	CHOTEAU, Marie Louise 30th, Bishop Dubourg	MOG 10 April 1818
PAYTON, John S.	CLINETINCH, Matulda 5 Nov., W. W. Kitzmiller, JP	MORE 10 Nov. 1849
PEART, Boanerges E. formerly Logan Co. KY	BAILEY, Sabra Caroline (2nd dau. of George, Esq.) of and at Logan Co., KY 1st inst., Rev. Stemmons	MORE 28 July 1841
PECK, Charles A. of St. Louis	POTTER, Adeline E. formerly of Leydon, MA at Cincinnati 8 March, Rev. Sehon	MORE 14 March 1842
PECK, Ruluph	STODDARD, Adeline (Dr. John) at Dardenne, St. Charles 19th, Rev. J. M. Peck	MOG 16 Feb. 1820
PEIXOTTO, D. C.	LEVY, Matilda (3rd dau. Michael) of NY City	SWERE 15 Dec. 1845
PEMBERTON, John	ELLIS, Mary at Monticello 20 Jan. 1847	PWH 4 Feb. 1847
PENRICE, John S. of Princeton, (MO? MS?)	LONG, Amelie of St. Louis n.d., Rev. N. Childs	MORE 14 May 1842

PERRY, R. P. of St. Louis	GRATTON, Margaretta of and at NY 17 Nov.	MORE 20 Nov. 1846
PESCAY, Julius	MERINOT, Angelica 22nd, Bishop Dubourg	SLINQ 30 Aug. 1826
PETTES, Eleazar P. of St. Louis	ATKINS, Emily (ygst. Capt. Isaiah) at Central Church, Boston n.d., Rev. Rogers	MORE 1 Nov. 1842
PETTIBONE, Henry	McELROY, Margaret near Bowling Green 7 April, Rev. James Campbell	MORE 18 April 1847
PETTINGILL, Daniel	BICKMORE, Anna at Madison Co. IL 27th ult, Joseph Meacham, Esq.	MOG 22 Jan. 1819
PEUGNET, Lewis D. of New York	ALEXANDER, Mrs. Theresa (Gen. H. Pratte of St. Louis) at Philadelphia	MORE 2 March 1830
PEYRAU (Peyron?), Faben	ARMSTRONG, Mary Ann 26 July, Rev. Alex Van Court	SWERE 31 July 1848
PHILIPS, Capt. Joseph	MORRISON, Elouisa (Capt. Wm.) at Kaskaskia, IL 24th, Rev. Fr. Oliver	MOG 30 Aug. 1817
PHILIPS, Thomas C. both from Co. Donegal	GRIERSON, Margaret 26th, Rev. Davis	BEA 28 June 1832
PHILLIPS, Edward J. of Springfield, IL	LEE, Martha of St. Louis 23rd inst., Rev. Early	MORE 30 Dec. 1834
PHILLIPS, Nathaniel of St. Louis	HARTSHORN, Harriet (Rolun, Esq.) at Boston 26 March	MORE 31 March 1846
PHILLIPS, Robert B. of St. Louis	BALDWIN, Anna Theresa (David) of and at Perry, IL 8 May, Rev. VanCleve	MORE 12 May 1850
PIERCE, Peter of Boonville	TURNER, Mary of Howard Co. Tues. last, Rev. Patton	BOLT 29 Oct. 1842
PILKINGTON, Samuel B.	MULFORD, Elizabeth 31 Dec., Rev. Weed	SWERE 3 Jan. 1847

PLUMP, Col. Erich of Jefferson City	SPEAR, Julia M. at Leicester, Mass. 28 May	JINQ 19 June 1845
POCOCKE, William M.	McGHEE, Caroline Thurs. last, no minister given (Rev. Horrell, BEA 30 Sept.)	MORE 28 Sept. 1830
POGUE, Robert of Edwardsville, IL	SNOW, Lucinda of St. Louis 29th, Rev. DeAndreis	MOG 11 Aug. 1819
POLLOCK, James of Illinois	CONWAY, Ann (Capt.) of Bonhomme, St. L. Co. n. d., Rev. Salmon Giddings	MORE 25 Dec. 1822
POPE, Orris	SUTTON, Frances 26 Dec., Wm. R. Walker, Esq.	PWH 8 Jan. 1845
POPE, R. B.	WISE, Ann Eliza of St. Louis, at Fairfield, Iowa 27 Oct., Rev. D. S. Smith	MORE 2 Nov. 1850
PORTER, James H.	HARRIS, Amelia (A.O.) of and at Memphis, TN 25 July, Episcopal Church Rev. G. W. Sill	SWERE 7 Aug. 1848
POSTON, Milton both of St. Francois Co.(?)	BERKLEY, Ann Elizabeth 4th, Rev. John F. Cowan	MORE 11 April 1844
POTTER, John C.	YOSTI, Marie 2 April	MOG 10 April 1818
POWELL, Joseph	WILSON, Ellen(late James of Philadelphia) Tuesday, Rev. Potts	MORE 21 Aug. 1832
POWELL, Peter merchant of St. Louis	WILSON, Jane (James) of and at Philadelphia 10th, Rev. James P. Wilson	MORE 6 May 1828
POWELL, William of St. Louis	ROBINS, Mary W. (Thomas) at Philadelphia 6th, Rev. Thos. Clark	HORL 20 Nov. 1845
POWERS, William	BAILEY, Mrs. Atalanta at Monroe Co., 9th	MORE 15 Oct. 1823
PRAGOFF, William	HARKINS, Mrs. Mary of Cincinnati 23 Aug., Rev. Bullard	MORE 27 Aug. 1838
PRATHER, J. V.	BOOKER, Henrietta Maria (Maj. Wm.) of Springfield, KY 10th inst., Rev. J. T. Jarboe	MORE 19 June 1846

PRICE, Christopher M. of St. Louis	KYLE, Harriet of Catauba, near Fincastle at Fincastle, VA 1 Dec. 1818	MOG 8 Jan. 1819
PRICE, John of Baltimore Co., MD	PRICE, Ann (Risdon, Esq.) 5th inst., Rev. Thos. Howell	MORE 6 Oct. 1843
PRICE, Capt. Risdon H.	BISSELL, Mary (Brig. Gen.) Wed. last	MOG 26 Aug. 1815
PRICKETT, Abraham merchant of Edwardsville, IL	HARRIS, Martha also of Edwardsville Thurs.	MOG 16 May 1821
PRIESTLY, Dr. ____ of Jonesborough, IL	BREVARD, Margaret (Robert) of Cape Girardeau Co. Scott Co., 26th	MORE 14 June 1831
PROCTOR, Dr. W. H. all of Bloomington, MO	BAIRD, Mrs. Mary ; 7th inst., Rev. I. B. Allen	GLWT 14 April 1853
PROVER, Robert J.	WEBSTER, Catherine 25th inst., Moses Taylor, JP	MORE 28 July 1848
PULLIAM, Capt. Wm. M.	THRALL, Minerva (late A.) 25th, Rev. M. V. Payne	COMB 9 Dec. 1847
PURDIN, William	PATTERSON, Miss ____ in Boonville "last Tuesday" Rev. Just. Williams	MIN 24 Oct. 1828
PURKY, P. M.	GREATHOUSE, Eliza Jane Ralls Co., the 15th	BGBD 22 April 1845
PUTNEY, Amos C.	NEWTON, Martha Ann 27th, Rev. Goodrich	MORE 29 Oct. 1847
QUARLES, Dr. Pryor	EASTON, Joanna A. (Col. Rufus) Thurs. last, Rev. Giddings	MOG 6 Sept. 1817
RADFORD, Lt. Wm. U.S.N.	LOVELL, Mary (only, Joseph, Esq.) at St. Peter's Church Morristown, NJ 21 Dec., Rev. Chas. Rankin	MORE 8 Jan. 1849
RAGAN, George of Hannibal	WILSON, Louise J. n.d., Rev. John Young	PWH 6 Aug. 1845
RAGSDALE, Richard	DEAVER, Elizabeth 18 June, Rev. Bell	MORE 3 July 1832
RALPH, George W.	HAY, Elizabeth (John, Esq.) at Belleville, IL 5 Feb., Rev. Lutz	SOV 9 Feb. 1833

RANDALL, John D. of Baltimore, MD	ACKLEY, Hannah Thurs., Rev. Tabor	MORE 6 Sept. 1831
RANKIN, Capt. T. M. U. S. Army St. Charles	WALLER, Mary Amelia of Louisville, KY at West Philadelphia Scott. Co.(?), 17 April at res. Wm. Rodgers, Esq.	MORE 29 April 1839
RANNELLS, Charles, Esq. of St. Louis	WARDER, Mary A. (Jeremiah) at Springfield, Ohio 19 May	MORE 1 June 1842
RANSOM, S. H. of Albany, NY	SANFORD, Virginia E. (Alexander) Rev. Horrell, the 11th	HORL 18 Dec. 1845
RAWLINGS, Hiram	ORME, Martha 24th inst., Rev. Chederton	MORE 1 Nov. 1833
RAY, Winthrop G.	CLAPP, Georgianna Wingate (Charles Q.), at Portland, ME 10th	HORL 27 Nov. 1845
READ, Dr. J. W.	EWING, Pamelia J. (Rev. Finis) 8th inst.,Just. Williams	MIN 18 April 1828
RECTOR, Stephen	LEE, Lydia (P.) of and at St. Charles, the 20th	MOG 27 Nov. 1818
REDMAN, Rev. Wm. Winn of Clark Co., Indiana	BURCKHARTT, Mary Ann 9th inst., Rev. Just. Williams	MIN 14 Oct. 1823
REED, Henry S. of St. Louis	PLATT, Angelina at Tremont, IL 12 Nov., Rev. Andrews	MORE 17 Nov. 1850
REED, John D.	THOMPSON, Margaret Sunday last	MOG 2 Dec. 1815
REED, John H. late of St. Louis	HEALDT, Fredericka of and at Little Rock, AR 16th inst.	MORE 28 Oct. 1834
REED, Joseph D.	RION, Margaret A. 16 Nov., Reed, JP	MORE 17 Nov. 1841
REEL, J. W. merchant of St. Louis	SHREVE, Harriet S.(eld. Capt.H.M.) of and at Louisville, KY 1st, Rev. D. C. Banks, Jr.	MORE 13 July 1830
REESE, David R. of Monticello, MO	MURDOCK, Elizabeth (late Wm.) at Boone Co., KY 14 May	MORE 6 June 1839

REILLY, J. P. of St. Louis	TAYLOR, Ann Elizabeth Paxton (eld. John) of and at Pittsburgh, 22 Feb., Rev. Garland	MORE 6 March 1844
REILLY, Capt. Robert A. of St. Louis	CORWITH, Phoebe R. (Gurdin, Esq.) of Bridgehampton, LI, NY 3 Feb., Rev. C. H. Edgar	SWERE 1 March 1847
REILY, Henry	PADDOCK, Julia at Locust Grove, IL 9th, Rev. Giddings	MORE 16 Aug. 1827
RENALS, William	DAYS, Polly Ann 1 Jan., Rev. Barnes	MIN 24 Jan. 1835
RENFREW, John of St. Louis	HAZELTON, Eliza formerly of Pittsburgh, at New Sharon, PA, 26th ult	MORE 26 Oct. 1837
RENSER, Isaac	LeFAIVRE, Pelagie 24 Nov., Rev. Heim	SWERE 29 Nov. 1847
RENSHAW, William merchant of St. Louis	KLEIN, Phoebe Ann Eliza (Joseph) late of Catskill, NY at Chesterfield Thurs., Rev. Ward	SLINQ 5 Feb. 1820
RENWICK, William	HOLMES, Elixa 22 April, Rev. Borgna	SOV 27 April 1833
REPPY, Henry G. of Missouri	CUMMINS, Elizabeth late of Ohio at Galena, IL 1 Jan., Rev. Wilcox	MORE 13 Jan. 1840
REYNOLDS, William T.	SPALDING, Julia (Josiah) at Christ Church last Wed., Rev. Horrell	SWERE 15 March 1847
RHODES, Jacob	MARION, Sarah E. formerly of Conn. the 24th	SLDU 1 March 1847
RICE, Anapias	STAMPS, Bettie (Thos.) of Bourbon, KY 12 Nov., Elder Thos. DuBar	MORE 6 Dec. 1850
RICE, William R.	GORDON, Sarah 17 April, Geo. W. Miller	JINQ 21 April 1838
RICHARDS, B. S. of Parkville	BROWNER, Cynthia A. of Brunswick 14th inst., Dr. Bull	GLWT 21 Oct. 1852

RICHARDS, Lewis	TYNNELL, Mrs.Jane near Chariton 13th inst., Rev. Eb. Rodgers	MIN 20 May 1823
RICHARDS, R. K. co-ed. St. Louis Times	LAMB, Matilda (Gen. Anthony) at New York City 30 Oct., Rev. Cor	MORE 27 Nov. 1832
RICHARDSON, Freeman of Boston	MURRAY, Mrs. Priscilla formerly of this city at Gretna, LA, 27 March Rev. Twickel	SWERE 16 April 1849
RICHMOND, Volney	WEST, Victoria at Madison Co., IL 22 April, Rev. Rogers	SWERE 26 April 1847
RIDER, Samuel of St. Louis	CARLDON, Angeline of and at Griggsville, IL 9th, Rev. Balland	MORE 18 Nov. 1843
RIDGELY, Franklin L.	ROBERT, Eleanor Tues. last, Rev. Horrell	MORE 24 March 1829
RIDGELY, Stephen	HILL, Susan L. at Upper Alton 20 April, Rev. G. Selleck	MORE 28 April 1840
RILEY, Major B. of the Army at Jefferson Barracks	ISRAEL, Miss____ late of Philadelphia 6th inst.	MORE 11 Nov. 1834
RILEY (?), John L.	BRADY, Widow at St. Charles the 5th	SCMO 12 Sept. 1822
RINGER, Matthias P. both of Carondelet vicinity	CONSTANT, Julia Ann (Gabriel) 22nd, John Bent, JP	BEA 26 April 1832
RISLEY, Luke of St. Louis	FOOT, Caroline of and at Marlborough, CT,n.d.	MORE 2 Feb. 1830
RISLY, David R. All of St. Louis (see RUBY)	BAILEY, Mrs. Margaret A. 30th ult.	MODE 12 Jan. 1848
RISQUE, Ferd. W., Esq.	PICKRELL, Caroline Saloma (John Esq.) at Georgetown, DC 13th inst., Rev. Shiras	MORE 22 Oct. 1846
RITCHIE, W. G. merchant, formerly of Madison, IN	LELAND, Maria A. (John D., judge 2nd Jud. Dist. MO) form. VA 23rd, Rev. Coulter	BOLT 27 April 1844
ROBIDOUX, Felix of and at Savannah, MO	SMITH, Jane C.S. recently of St. Louis 8 Dec., Rev. Carson	MORE 23 Nov. 1842

RODGERS, Rev. Ebenezer	JACKSON, Permelia 28th ult., Rev. John Bull	MIN 26 Aug. 1823
RODGERS, Jesse H.	SPENCER, Nancy Ann (Capt. Gideon) at Chesterfield 4th, Rev. Peck	MORE 7 June 1820
ROE, Joseph	BOYCE, Margaret last Thurs., Rev. Bailey	COMB 12 Oct. 1835
ROGERS, Capt. J. U. S. Army	PRESTON, Josephine (late Maj. Wm.) at Louisville 16th, Rev. Page	MORE 25 Oct. 1831
ROGERS, Joseph P. merchant of St. Louis	DAVIS, Mary Lewis (C.A.) of Carrollton, IL 29 June	MORE 1 July 1846
RONEY, Michael	MALLEY, Julia 9th, I. B. Thompson, JP	MORE 10 Oct. 1843
ROOKER,C. F. of Rockville, Iowa	ROOKER, Lutetia (Capt. John) 23rd	MODE 1 Dec. 1847
RORER, Samuel N. of Clay Co.	SNELL, Narcissa (Wm., decd.) 1st inst., Squire Swetnam	BOLT 7 Jan. 1843
RUBY, David R. all of St. Louis (see RISLY)	BAILEY, Margaret Al. 30 Dec., Rev. Creasey	COMB 13 Jan. 1848
RUNDLETT, John S. of St. Louis	WILLIAMS, Elizabeth M. (late Saml.) of and at Philadelphia 16 April, Rev. Skinner	MORE 4 May 1830
RUSH, James both of Lewis Co.	MARKS, Sarah M. (George) 15 Feb., Rev. John Monroe	PWH 19 Feb. 1842
RUSSELL, John B. editor of Iowa News	DAVIDSON, Frances of St. Louis, at Burlington, Iowa Terr., n.d., Hon. C. Mason	MORE 11 Feb. 1840
RUSSELL, Richard both of St. Louis Theatre	SYLVIA, Amelia 3 May	SWERE 4 May 1846
RUTLAND, James of Blandville, KY	RUTTER, Emily (John P.) 18 March, Rev. Rush	PWH 25 March 1847
RUTTER, James	HOLLYMAN, Mary Ann (Thomas) 15th, Rev. C. Gentry	PWH 24 Feb. 1844
RYLAND, Edwin M.	PEEBLES, Eliza in Franklin last Thursday	MIN 19 Dec. 1828

70

RYLAND, John F.	BUFORD, Elizabeth Gabriella (Maj. S.), formerly Frankfort,KY at Fairfield, Lafayette Co. 29 Sept., Rev. Yantis	MIN 17 Oct. 1835
SABIN, Elijah, Esq.	MATTHEWS, Mary Jane formerly of St. Louis at Leavenworth, IN 8 Oct., Rev. Samuel Weeks	MORE 22 Oct. 1849
ST. VRAIN, Felix	GREGOIRE, Mary (2nd of Charles) at Ste. Genevieve 30th Oct.	MORE 20 Nov. 1822
ST. VRAIN, S.	MENARD, Virginia (Maj. H.) n.d., at Kaskaskia	MORE 2 March 1830
SALISBURY, Philander	HUNTINGTON, Eliza Irena formerly of Randolph, VT 26th inst., Rev. Drummond	MORE 26 Sept. 1834
SAMUEL, Edward M. merchant of Liberty, Clay Co.	GARNER, Elizabeth E. (Col. J.W.) in Howard Co. 23 May, Rev. Hampton Boon	MIN 1 June 1833
SAMUEL, Giles M. of this city	CUMMINS, Letitia Wed.,last, Rev. Justinian Williams	MIN 7 Oct. 1823
SAMUEL, Presley all of this place	SHAW, Nancy (Capt. John) last Thurs., Rev. Just. Williams	MIN 18 Jan. 1826
SAMUEL, Thomas J.	GREEN, Mrs. Susan of Huntsville, the 6th	BRUNS 29 July 1848
SAMUEL, William P. of Franklin Co., KY	SHANNON, Sara Lavenia (late Judge George of St. Charles Co.) at Frankfort, KY 1 May, Rev. Thos. P. Dudley	MORE 16 May 1838
SANDER, John of Howard Co.	STINER, Charlotte E. of Boonville 23rd, Rev. Slocum	BOMO 28 May 1844
SANDS, S. G. of St. Louis	WRIGHT, Anna Maria C. (Thomas) late of Cincinnati at Camden, MO	OSD 21 April 1843
SANGUINETTE, Charles Jr.	BRAZEAU, Miss ____ n.d.	MOG 19 Oct. 1816
SAUNDERS, Daniel G. all of Chariton Co.	HIX, Laura A. 2nd, Rev. W. G. Caples	BOLT 13 Dec. 1845

SAVAGE, Rev. F.A.
of Mason Co., KY

MOSBY, Mary Jane
formerly of Lynchburg, VA
at res. Capt. W.D. Swinney
at Glasgow, Missouri
2nd, Rev. John Bull

BOLT
11 Nov. 1843

SAVAGE, Wm. H.
merchant of St. Louis

ADDISON, Anna Maria (Z. Huffman,
Esq.) at Red Rock, NY
30 June, Rev. Kettle

MORE
24 July 1832

SCHOEFFLER, Charles C.
of St. Louis

SAVER, Louisa
of and at Hennepin, IL
11th inst., Rev. Dickey

MORE
14 June 1849

SCOTT, Capt. Charles M.

GOODRICH, Miss E.A.
16 July, Rev. H. P. Goodrich

MORE
13 July 1840

SCOTT, John R.
of St. Louis

MILLER, Sarah C. (eld. late
Thomas) at Kent Co., MD
16th, St. Paul's Church,
Rev. Samuel Gordon

MORE
23 Feb. 1850

SCOTT, James

GAW, Elizabeth
Thurs. last, Rev. Just. Williams

MIN
14 May 1825

SCOTT, Dr. John W.

HOYT, Mary Ann (Hon. Noah)
formerly Utica, NY, at
Perkiman, Ohio, 17th

MOG
28 Nov. 1821

SCOTT, Lewis

BRANNIN, Elizabeth (Capt. Richard)
Thurs. last, Rev. Just. Williams

MIN
25 Jan. 1825

SCOTT, Samuel S.
of NY

McBETH, Angeline
of this city
23 July, Rev. A. Vancourt

SWERE
31 July 1848

SEARS, Rev. Arthur E.
of Mo. Annual Conference

HAWKINS, Julia A. (James C.)
of and at Shelbyville
n.d. (PWH 20 April says 17 April)

BRUNS
27 April 1848

SEBREE, Laban
of this place

EDWARDS, Miranda B. (Rev. John)
of Clay Co.
15th inst., Rev. Hill

BOLT
24 Sept.1842

SEDGWICK, Selser
of St. Louis

HOUSTON, Sarah Ann
of and at Louisville
15th, Rev. D. C. Banks

MORE
23 June 1837

SEELY, C. C.
of Pittsburgh

MEANS, Eliza C.
of Missouri, at Greensburgh, PA
26th, Rev. R. Henry

MORE
10 Aug. 1830

SEHON, Rev. Edward

McLEAN, Miss ____ (William)
of and at Cincinnati
4th inst

MORE
8 Sept. 1833

SELKIRK, Alexander   JOHNSTONE, Louisa A.   MORE
                           28th inst., Rev. Neils(?)   30 Oct. 1847

SELLERS, Capt. Isaiah   WELCH, Amanda M. F.   MORE
of St. Louis   of Frankford, KY at   10 Aug. 1838
                           res. Jesse Pell, Smithland, KY
                           7 July, Rev. Willis

SELLS, Walter   BRIGGS, Mrs. Kate   MORE
both formerly of Ohio   n.d., Rev. Chas. Summerville   1 Aug. 1850

SETTLE, Wm. H.   EVANS, Harriet D. (only, Evan) SWERE
1st clerk on steamboat   in Frankfort, KY   29 Nov. 1847
George Washington   18 Nov., Rev. Bullock

SEXTON, James   FORD, Ann (Edward)   MIN
of Boone Co.   of Montgomery Co.   19 March 1830
                           8 March, Rev. Wm. Crain

SHACKELFORD, Richard   HUBBARD, Ann (late Dr. J.)   MIN
of Boonville   at Howard Co.   13 March 1824
                           Wed., Rev. Just. Williams

SHACKELFORD, Richard C.   SCOTT, Ann Maria Caroline   MORE
of Hannibal   (Jefferson) of Bourbon, KY   21 Oct. 1846
                           at Lexington, KY 14 Oct.
                           Rev. G. Moore

SHANNON, A. J.   BRITTON, Emma L. (A.)   SPAD
of Neosho   at Jasper Co.   19 Sept. 1846
                           2 Sept., Rev. Patterson

SHARP, Dr. Benjamin F.   McGHEE, Mary   MORE
of Danville, MO   late of Shelbyville, KY   2 Oct. 1840
                           at Danville, 22 Sept.
                           Rev. Lester James

SHARP, William   DEAUGHERTY, Mrs. Elizabeth   MORE
                           9 Dec., I.B. Thomas, JP   11 Dec. 1841

SHAW, Lyman B.   RIDGELY, Octavia (Noah)   MORE
                           of and at Baltimore, MD   7 April 1834
                           10th, Rev. Henshaw

SHAW, Robert   DUNCAN, Mary (Daniel, Esq.)   MIN
merchant of Franklin   at Paris, KY, 13 Feb.   18 March 1823

SHAW, Thomas   CROSS, Mary Josephine   MORE
of Commerce, MO   of and at Ste. Genevieve   16 Nov. 1837
                           31st ult, Rev. Beard

SHELTON, Charles D.   HAMMOND, Mary Jane (Robt., Esq.) MORE
                           at Oak Grove (IL?), 26th   9 March 1846
                           Elder Thos. Wright
                                                           73

SHEPARD, Elihu H. of St. Louis	THOMAS, Mary of and at Belleville,IL 10th, Rev. Mitchel	MORE 13 Aug. 1823
SHEPARD, John B. of St. Louis	ACHLAND, Sarah Ann (eld. James, Esq.) at Baltimore 2nd inst.	MORE 12 Feb. 1846
SHEPHERD, George Washington of this place	HIX, Julia A. at Chariton (Co.?) 26 Nov., Rev. John Bull	MIN 11 Dec. 1829
SHEPHERD, James M.	CONWAY, Sarah Howard Co.?, n.d.	MORE 22 Feb. 1831
SHEPPARD, Joseph M.	CONWAY, Sarah (Thos., Esq.) 27 Jan., Rev. Bull	MIN 12 Feb. 1831
SHEPHERDSON, Jno. K.	DURNO, Margaret 1st inst., Rev. Lewis	MORE 4 Feb. 1849
SHORT, Evin. of Miller Co.	JONES, Nancy Ann at Pulaski Co. 19 Dec., Rev. Isaac Clark	JINQ 13 Jan. 1842
SHORTRIDGE, Dr. Wm. T. of Fulton, MO	BARTLETT, Thomasella V. of and at Lexington, KY 2nd inst.	MORE 11 May 1849
SHREVE, Capt. H. M.	ROGERS, Lydia R. (late Capt. John W.) of Boston, in Louisville, 28 Nov.	MORE 3 Dec. 1846
SHURLDS, Henry Attorney	BURT, Jane J. of and at Potosi, MO 14 March	MORE 3 April 1822
SIBLEY, George C.	EASTON, Mary (Col. Rufus)	MOG 16 Sept. 1815
SILVERBURG, Robert	SAMUEL, Clara 17 Aug., Justice Spalding	MORE 19 Aug. 1850
SINGLE, Benjamin	BOSWELL, Jane (Charles) of St. Louis, at Bell Falls, WI 23 Aug.	MORE 26 Sept. 1849
SISSON, Edward late of Louisville, KY	JONES, Cynthia Ann (eld. John) at St. Ferdinands, St. L. Co. n.d., Rev. Shumate	MORE 20 Aug. 1842
SLADE, Wm. M. all of Rocheport, Boone Co.	PHILLIPS, Susan (Wm.) Tues. last, Rev. A. B. Hardy	BOLT 16 March 1844

SLAUGHTER, Thomas J. of Independence	HENRY, Mary of and at Louisville, KY 3rd inst., Rev. E. Humphrey	INJUN 19 Sept. 1844
SLOANE, J. M. all of Elkhorn, Washington Co.	HOOD, Mary 15 April, Rev. Wm. Sloan	MORE 28 April 1847
SMALL, Capt. Joel	KELLY, Ann C. (Moses, Esq.) of Pike Co. n.d., Rev. Wm. F. Watson	MORE 27 Sept. 1850
SMARR, Abner	FIELDS, Caroline B. 16 Dec., Rev. C. S. Turner	PWH 1 Jan. 1846
SMILEY, Alfred	HALL, Lucinda at res. Garrard Banks nr. Houston, 9 Aug., Rev. Elias Leach	PWH 20 Aug. 1845
SMITH, Benj. of Fayette	HUNTINGTON, Martha at res. of B.C. Webster, Springfield, IL 27th, Rev. Dresser	BOLT 5 April 1845
SMITH, Dalzell merchant of St. Louis	THOME, Mary (Arthur) at Augusta, KY 12 Sept., Rev. Tomlinson	MOAR 23 Sept. 1836
SMITH, I. T. all late of VA	BARTHALOW, Ann E. at Howard Co. 24th inst., Rev. Joel Prewitt	MORE 28 Jan. 1843
SMITH, J. Perrine of St. Louis	BAKER, Susan (Wm., Esq.) of and at Medina, NY 6 Aug., Rev.Stokes	MORE 22 Aug. 1840
SMITH, James C. all of our neighborhood	BOONE, Melcina 13th inst., N. Forry	WEJO 15 Feb. 1845
SMITH, James R.	JAMES, Angeline (eld. C.W.) at Cincinnati 16th inst., Rev. Lynd	MORE 24 May 1843
SMITH, John merchant of St. Louis	McDOUGAIL, Louisa A. (late Alex.) of and at New York 19th June	SLINQ 26 July 1826
SMITH, Lewis of Chariton Co.	WILSON, Martha Ann of Howard Co. 6th, Rev. L. Robiou	BOLT 12 Sept. 1840
SMITH, Oliver C. merchant	LEE, Jemima all of this city, 23rd	MOG 6 Oct. 1819
SMITH, Capt.Robert	DAMERON, Martha (Wm. M., decd.) 20th, Rev. Silas Williams	BOLT 29 April 1843

SMITH, Wm. formerly Norfolk, VA	SINGLETON, Anna (Henry) 16th, Rev. Minard	MORE 18 May 1839
SMYZER, George of Missouri	WILLSON, Martha A. of MD at res. Thomas Willson, Montgomery Co., MD. 11 Aug., Rev. Henry Slicer	MORE 20 Aug. 1847
SNOW, Henry H. of Quincy, IL	KNIGHT, Lucy of and at Westmoreland, NH 1 Aug.	MORE 27 Sept. 1827
SNYDER, Jacob both of Illinois	JONES, Mrs. Ursula Thurs., John R. Gay	SLINQ 7 June 1820
SOMES, Joseph, MD	VANDERBURGH, Frances Sydney (late Judge) at Vincennes n.d., Rev. Shea	MORE 20 Dec. 1831
SOULARD, James G. merchant	HUNT, Eliza M. n.d., Rev. duBourg	MOG 22 March 1820
SOUTHACK, Francis of St. Louis, formerly of Boston	LOTT, Emelina Louisa formerly of Trenton, NJ at St. John's Ch., Quincy, IL 11 June, Rev. Hodges	MORE 15 June 1839
SOUTHERLAND, George	ELLINGTON, Mrs. E. at Jefferson Co. n.d., Rev. Gilbreath	SLDU 7 Sept. 1846
THOMPSON, Peter J. merchant of Palmyra	THOMPSON, Mary P. of and at Kanawha Salines, VA 20 April	PWH 7 May 1842
SPARR, _____ . Esq.	DREW, Sarah (Dr. C.) late of Camden, _ 18th ult., J. D. Snider	MORE 3 Jan. 1838

(This newspaper has been damaged)

SPENCER, Charles L. merchant of Santa Fe	PARKER, Mary E. (eld. N.W., Esq.) 7 May, Rev. N. Childs, Jr.	MORE 9 May 1850
SPENCER, John W.	CASE, Louisa M. at Morgan Co., IL 17th ult., Rev. Simms	MORE 6 May 1828
SPENCER, Dr. M. C. both of this neighborhood	ELLIOTT, Mrs.May n.d., no minister	BRUNS 14 Oct. 1848
SPRATT, G. W.	COWEN, Henrietta Frances (eld., Hyman) 30 Aug., Van Bakelen	MORE 31 Aug. 1849

STAGG, Edward	DAGGETT, Harriet H.(John D.) at St. Louis, Sun. last Bishop Kemper	BOLT 4 April 1840
STAHL, Nicholas of Galena, IL	BEEBE, Sarah A. of St. Louis 1 Oct., Rev. Potts	MORE 3 Oct. 1844
STANHOPE, John B., Jr. of Ohio	WAITE, Louisa (late Saml. Coates of NY), St. John's Church n.d., Rev. Griswold	MORE 22 March 1849
STARK, Horatio	PENNEMAN, Mrs. Eliza 16 June	MOG 24 July 1813
STARK, William of Jefferson City	LEWIS, Sophronia (late Edmond) of Chariton, 7 Nov.	BRUNS 11 Nov. 1848
STARR, Wm. E. of St. Louis	STEPHENSON, Elvira Amanda (late Col. Benj.), Thurs. Thos. Lippincott, at Edwardsville, IL	MORE 22 March 1827
STAVELY, John W. of Shelbyville	INGRAHAM, Catherine G. of Palmyra Tues. last, Rev. John Orrange	PWH 10 Oct. 1840
STEINFELD, John Esq. all of Boonville	RICKETTS, M. Louisa Mon. evening, Rev. N. Childs	MORE 29 Oct. 1844
STEPHENS, James L.	HOCKADAY, Amelia (Judge J.O.) at Columbia 7 Feb., Rev. Isaac Jones	MORE 17 Feb. 1844
STEPHENSON, Col. James W. of Galena, IL	KYLE, Ellen (David) yesterday, Rev. Chaderton	MORE 12 Dec. 1834
STETTINIUS, Joseph of St. Louis	MAXWELL, Adeline (late Hugh H.) of (and at?) Kaskaskia 7th inst., Rev. Perrin	MORE 10 Aug. 1849
STEUART, A. D. Paymaster, U.S. Army	ATKINSON, Mary (late Thomas Bullitt), St. John's Church, Washington, 5 March, Rev. Hawley	MORE 15 March 1844
STEVENS, Charles W., MD	DILLON, Susan F. (Patrick, Esq.) 10 Oct., no minister	MORE 13 Oct. 1844
STEVENS, R. H., MD U. S. Army	CORDELL, Missouri Ann (H., Esq.) 15th inst., Rev. Hiram Goodrich	MORE 26 Oct. 1846
STEWART, Dr. A.	AYRES, Emily (Ebenezer) "at forks of the Missouri" Sat. eve. last, Rev. Timothy Flint	MOG 3 Aug. 1816

STEWART, Thomas J.
of St. Louis

GARDINER, Melani Veron
(2nd dau. of Baldwin)
at New York, 29 June
Rev. Orville Dewey

MORE
13 July 1834

STEWART, Major William

SOUTHWICK, Mary Jane (Danl. H.)
formerly of Boston
5th inst., Rev. Fr____?

MORE
7 Jan. 1846

STICKNEY, Benjamin
of St. Louis

HUNTER, Lucy
of and at Boonville, NY
8th inst.

MORE
24 Oct. 1846

STOCKER, William H.

MATHEWS, Mary M.
31 Jan., Rev. Goodrich

MORE
1 Feb. 1847

STOCKTON, Richard G.
of Lexington, MO

MORTON, Ann (George, Esq.)
late of Lexington, KY
30 Jan., Rev. Johnson, M.E. Church

MORE
19 Feb. 1844

STOKES, William

NESTER, Nancy
Thurs., Sears, JP

BOLT
30 Oct. 1841

STONE, Wm. Esq.
of Ralls Co.

RIDDLE, Catherine B.
2nd, Rev. Hayes

PWH
23 Oct. 1845

STOUT, Benj. F.
of St. Louis

THOMPSON, Delia A. (John, Esq.)
at Bridgeport, CT
15 Sept., Rev. Hunter

MORE
29 Sept. 1847

STREET, George W.

ALLEGA, Talitha
at Howard Co., the 26th

BRUNS
30 Sept. 1848

STROTHER, George F.
of St. Louis

HUNT, Theodocia L. (John W.,Esq.) MORE
at Lexington, KY
2 June

20 June 1825

STUART, Charles W.

HART, Ann (Samuel L.)
Wednesday, Rev. Pierce

JINQ
3 Nov. 1838

STUART, W. H. H.

POWELL, Ann M.
formerly of Paris, KY
at St. Mary's Landing, MO
11th, Rev. Jno. T. Pierce

MORE
15 July 1844

SULLIVAN, Geo. W.
of St. Louis Co.

VIRDEN, Anne S. (Samuel)
of Kent Co., Del., at St. Louis
15th, Rev. Horrell

MORE
18 Feb. 1848

SUMMERS, Maston T.
all of Parkville, Platte Co.

BEEDING, America (C.P.)
7th, Rev. Calomel

GLWT
21 Oct. 1852

SWITZER, Wm. N.

78

PREWITT, Mary Jane (Joel, Esq.)
in St. Louis, of Fayette
24th ult, Rt. Rev. Bishop Hawks

MODE
31 March 1847

SWON, John C. of St. Louis	KENNETT, Nancy K. of and at Carrollton, IL 21st, Saml. C. Pierce, Esq.	MORE 30 March 1830
TABOR, Dr. E. A.	FRISTOE, Elizabeth at Chariton 16 May, Rev. John Bull	MIN 20 June 1835
TAYLOR, Capt. Daniel of St. Louis	HENRIE, Angelique of Prairie du Rocher, IL 3rd inst., Esq. Brewer	MORE 10 July 1849
TAYLOR, Dubart M.	HUTCHINGS, Eliza (ygr. of John, Esq.) of Bellevue Washington Co. 16th, Cowan	MORE 24 May 1843
TAYLOR, John Holmes	GALASPE, Ellen Ann 18 June, Rev. Corson	MORE 3 July 1832
TAYLOR, Jeremiah R. of Monroe Co.	McLEON, Ellen Elizabeth (Dr. W.M.) MORE Randolph Co. (IL?) 23 Aug., Rev. Samuel Bruggs	3 Sept. 1839
TAYLOR, John H. of Saline Co.	CAMPBELL, Mary E. (J.) 3rd	COMB 26 Nov. 1847
TAYLOR, John S., Jr.	TAYLOR, Emily 30 Jan., Rev. G. A. Carrell	MORE 2 Feb. 1845
TAYLOR, Johnson of Montgomery Co.	CANTER, Edith of Femme Osage, St. Charles 9th, Rev. Craig	SLINQ 28 June 1820
TAYLOR, Joseph M. both late of Louisville	WATERFIELD, Martha A. 24 Oct., Rev. Tabor	MORE 30 Oct. 1839
TAYLOR, Levi late of Philadelphia	LaBARGE, Margaret 7th, Rev. Lutz	MORE 19 July 1836
TAYLOR, Nathaniel P. of Jefferson Co., KY	WALKER, Mrs. Matilda (Maj. Wm. Christy) Sun. last, Rev. Davis	MORE 26 June 1832
TAYLOR, Thomas	CAMPBELL, Sarah (James) 1 Dec., Rev. Cochran	PWH 5 Dec. 1840
TAYLOR, Thomas J.	COOK, Sarah J. (Col. Nath'l) of St. Francois Co., at res. Wm. Madden, Elk Grove, W.T. 4 Oct., D. G. Fenton, Esq.	MORE 20 Oct. 1838
TAYLOR, Thomas J.	WARD, Laura B. at Potosi, Washington Co. 24 June, Rev. D. Bainbridge	HORL 17 July 1845

TAYLOR, Thomas M.	COLLET, Emma S. (only of late Robert) at res. J. N. Macklot, Esq., Davenport, Iowa 25 Aug., Rev. Gold	MORE 7 Sept. 1847
TAYLOR, Capt. W. W.	KEATING, Martha 24th ult., Rev. Linn	MORE 3 Feb. 1849
TEETER, Gerrard	CREASON, Mary 27th ult, Boone Co.	MIN 9 Sept. 1823
TELEE, L. M. F.	LEBRUN, Louise of St. Louis, at Ft. Hyacinthe Lower Canada 28 April, Rev. Fonbon	MORE 29 April 1840
TEMPLAR, Louis	CLOY, Rosina Ann 16 Nov., Benj. McKenny	MORE 17 Nov. 1850
TERRILL, James H.	TURNER, Catherine Ann of Warren Twp. 13 Feb., Rev. S. S. McConnell	PWH 22 Feb. 1840
THATCH, T. H.	AULD, Zipporah W. 13 Dec., Rev. Pollock	MORE 16 Dec. 1849
THAYER, S. F. both of St. Louis	WATKINS, Sarah A. at Baltimore 4 Oct., Rev. Fuller	MORE 16 Oct. 1849
THOLOZAN, J. Eli	SANGUINET, Adele Tues. last	MOG 8 Jan. 1819
THOMAS, Ezra	ATCHISON, Elizabeth Thurs., Rev. _____	MORE 6 March 1832
THOMAS, Jesse B. of Galena, IL	SMITH, Adeline (Judge T. W.) at Edwardsville, IL n.d.	MORE 2 March 1830
THOMPSON, James P. both of St. Louis	DILLER, Sarah E. (Capt. J.) at Louisville 18 Nov., Rev. Jackson	MORE 25 Nov. 1841
THOMPSON, Col. John W.	LEE, B. 17th	MOG 23 March 1816
THOMPSON, Capt. Wildes T. of NM	DAVIS, Abby Low of St. Louis, in New Orleans 11th inst	MORE 21 July 1846
THORNBURGH, Josiah, Esq. of St. Louis	McCOLLOCH, Nancy M. (John,Esq.) of and at Wheeling, VA 26th, Rev. Holmes	MORE 27 March 1849

80

THORNBURG, William A. of St. Louis	CHAPMAN, Fanny Folger in New York 4 Oct., Rev. S. A. Corey	MORE 14 Oct. 1849
THORNTON, John of Franklin	TRIGG, Elizabeth (Col. Stephen) late of Estill Co., KY last Thursday	MIN 11 Feb. 1820
THROCKMORTON, Capt. J. of St. Louis	GORMON, Mary Jane of and at Pittsburgh 29th inst., Rev. John O'Reilly	MORE 12 Oct. 1836
TILLMAN, Charles of St. Louis	WADDLE, F. of and at Cahokia, IL 4 March, Rev. Loisel	MORE 6 May 1842
TILTON, William P.	HAY, Virginia (John) at Belleville, IL Tuesday	MORE 4 Oct. 1833
TODD, Albert, Esq. of St. Louis	WILSON, Jane (Gould) of and at Little Falls 27 Oct., Rev. Livermore	MORE 15 Nov. 1842
TODD, Ira	HARRIS, Minerva (John)	MODE 24 Feb. 1847
TOMPKINS, Benj. of Boonville	CLARK (ygst. late Gov. James of Kentucky), at St. Louis 11th inst., Bishop Hawks	GLWT 18 Nov. 1852
TOMPKINS, George	CATON, Mary 4 April, Rev. Goodrich	MORE 11 April 1844
TOOLEY, Porter	MUNRO, Ellen (eld., William) Thurs. last, Just. Williams	MIN 24 July 1824
TOWNSEND, Benjamin F. of St. Louis	WOOD, Lucinda (Thos., Esq. Of PA) at Green Co., IL 1 Jan.	MORE 6 Jan. 1845
TOWNSEND, James of St. Louis	CARNS, Adelaide G. (Peter A. of Baltimore) at New Albany, IN 21 Aug., Samuel Wilson, JP	MORE 8 Aug. 1844
TRABUE, Joseph of Glasgow, KY	MULLINS, Judith E. (only of Dr. L. G. of Warsaw, MO) At Greenville Inst., Harrodsburg, KY, 8th ult., President Shannon	MORE 7 Dec. 1842
TRACY, Alfred	STODDARD, Sarah (Dr. John) of St. Charles, at St. Louis Thurs. last, Rev. Cochran	MORE 27 May 1828

TRACY, Alfred	MORTON, Ellen (Geo., Esq.) Thurs. eve. last, Rev. Chaderton	MOAR 14 Aug. 1835
TRACY, Charles F.	MORTON, Sophia (Geo., Esq.) 19 Oct., Rev. Horrell	SWERE 25 Oct. 1847
TRAEGER, Charles August	ROBINSON, Catherine Elizabeth 13 July, Rev. Hurley	PWH 29 July 1847
TROWBRIDGE, George	McCARTAN, Sarah A. (late Thos.) 15th, Bishop Hawks	MORE 16 Nov. 1848
TULL, Thomas W.	STARKS, Leonice 3 Sept., Rev. W. P. Cochran	PWH 5 Sept. 1840
TURCOTTE, Narcisse of St. Louis	PREMBLAY, Adelline at St. Clair Co., IL n.d., Rev. Regis Loiselle	MORE 8 May 1839
TURNER, J. B. of St. Louis	RIPPEY, Mary of and at Monticello 24 March	MORE 31 March 1846
TURNER, Jos. P.	PARROT, Matilda M. 3rd inst., Rev. W. G. Elliott	HORL 11 Dec. 1845
TURPIN, Wm. R. merchant of Louisiana, MO	ROWND, Ann Morris of and at Philadelphia 26th ult, Rev. James P. Wilson	MORE 22 April 1828
TUTTLE, Gilpin	MOSS, Sarah (eld., Mason) in Boone Co., n.d.	MIN 31 Dec. 1822
TWICHELL, S., Esq. of New Orleans	WHITE, Mary L. of and at St. Louis, at Capt. Twichell n.d., Bishop Hawks	MORE 18 Oct. 1848
USHER, Samuel W. all of Chariton Co.	SPORTSMAN, Mary Ann (Abram) Wednesday	BRUNS 9 Dec. 1848
VAN BIBBER, Ewing	COURTNEY, Sarah at St. Charles 26 Nov., Jabez Hain(?)	MOAR 11 Dec. 1835
VAN DEVANTER, Wm. merchant of St. Louis	BISHOP, Harriet of and at New York City 27th, Rev. Sommers	MORE 17 Aug. 1837
VANDEVENTER, P. L. of St. Louis	WALLS, Emily (Capt. James) at Newport, KY 26 Nov., Rev. Riggon	MORE 5 Dec. 1844

VANDEVER, G. P. of Cooper Co., MO	LOVING, Malinda (John) of St. Louis, at 4th St. ME Ch. 29th inst., Rev. Hening	MORE 30 May 1849
VANHORN(?), Nathan	WHEELER, Mathilda C. (John B. of German Twp.) Sun., Rev. Flint	INP ____ March 1821
VANLANDINGHAM, Samuel	FREEMAN, Nancy in Marion Co. 29 Aug., Rev. Hayes	MORE 2 Sept. 1850
VANLANDINGHAM, Wm. of Knox Co.	MAXEY, Rebecca Jane Elizabeth Martha Ann (Boaz) in Monroe Co., 28 March Elder Henry Thomas	PWH 29 March 1849
VAN NORTWICK, Ira editor this paper	WARE, Mary Anne in Cooper Co. at Boonville 27th, Rev. J. J. Slocum	BORE 12 Dec. 1843
VANDIVER, John W. of Shelby Co.	JACOB, Julia Ann (John W.) of and at Romney, Hampshire Co.VA 11 Nov., Rev. A. D. Chenoweth	PWH 11 Dec. 1845
VANSANT, Isaiah	PASTUER, Virginia Ann of St. Louis, at New Orleans 10th inst.	MORE 14 Jan. 1842
VANVECHTEN, Abraham of Albany, NY	HAMILTON, Eliza M. of St. Louis, at Springfield, Mass. n.d.	MORE 18 Oct. 1842
VEITCH, Isaac McKendree	HERRICK, Henrietta K. (S.H.,Esq.) 4th St. ME Church 17th inst., Rev. J. Boyle	MORE 19 March 1844
VICARS, John formerly Baltimore and England	WORKMAN, Agnes Mon., Rev. Justinian Williams	MIN 26 June 1824
VICOREY, Francis M. of Macon Co.	BOZARTH, Elenora (Johnathan) of Howard Co. 5th, Justice Hanna	BOLT 14 Jan. 1843
VINCENT, Henry	HILL, Ann 3 Dec., Justice Hyde	MORE 4 Dec. 1840
VIVION, Flavel of Dover, Lafayette Co.	CHRISMAN, Mrs. Catherine of Fayette 17th, Rev. H. L. Boon	BOLT 23 July 1842
VIZZELL, Jacob	CORD, Amelia 8 Dec., McKenney, JP	MORE 10 Dec. 1850

VOLKER, Michael	KAESER, Verena 12 Oct., Cruess	MORE 28 Dec. 1844
VON SCHRADER, Frederick of Prussia	MORISON, Olivia of and at Kaskaskia IL 27 Aug., Fr. Roux	MORE 31 Aug. 1838
WADE, Capt. John M.	PEYTON, Harriet Jane formerly of VA n.d., Rev. J. C. Linn at res. Maj. W. C. Anderson	MORE 15 Aug. 1844
WALES, Dexter T. of St. Louis	BECKWITH, Caroline (late Capt. M.L.) at Louisville 12th, Rev. Humphrey	MORE 17 June 1844
WALKER, George A. all of Farmington	MURPHY, Jane T. n.d., Rev. Andrew Pease	MORE 31 Oct/1 Nov 1848
WALKER, James B. (John R.)	SULLIVAN, Mary (only, late John C.) 11 Feb., Rev. Hutchinson	MORE 15 Feb. 1847
WALKER, Orange all of Stillwater	LOCKWOOD, Georgianna E. 16 Nov. 1848, Rev. Boutwell	MORE 24 Jan. 1849
WALLACE, Hamilton W.	MACKLOT, Marie Isabelle (John N.) at Davenport, Iowa 15 June	MORE 23 June 1847
WALSH, James	FRENY, Mrs. Anastasia 3rd, Rev. Lutz	SOV 7 Feb. 1834
WALTON, John	POOL, Elizabeth at Sarcoxie, Jasper Co. 1st inst., Rev. Hinton	SPAD 7 March 1846
WARBURTON, John of St. Louis	SMITH, Mary Ann (Luther) of Hartford, CT, in New York City 14th, Rev. Ludlow	MORE 9 Nov. 1830
WARD, Porter of Norfolk, Eng.	WILD, Anna of Lancashire, Eng. 31 Dec., Rev. Pollock	MORE 4 Jan. 1847
WARDEN, John (see WARREN)	TRAINER, Mary Ana 11th, Fr. Hamilton	SLDU 15 Feb. 1847
WARNOCK, Mr. ____	McCLURE, Jane at Harrison, Illinois Territory "a few days ago"	MOG 19 April 1817
WARREN, John (see Warden)	TRAINER, Mary Ann 11 Feb., Rev. Fr. Hamilton	MORE 13 Feb. 1847

84

WARREN, Robert E. of St. Louis	HALL, Timothia Ann (Mrs. C. Hall of Vicksburg) "at Mrs. Hall's ranch" Upper Sacramento Valley 22 May	MORE 31 July 1850
WASHBURN, Lewis	HOWARD, Elizabeth Flora 14 July, D. Wetmore	SWERE 19 July 1847
WATERS, Absolem	OSGOOD, Marcella 1 Sept., McKenney, JP	MORE 2 Sept. 1849
WATERS, Samuel	MOORE, Elizabeth 21 Apr., I.B. Thomas, JP	MORE 23 Sept. 1841
WATKINS, Gen. Nathan W. of Jackson, MO	WATSON, Margaret (eld. Robert G., merchant) of and at New Madrid 5th inst.	MORE 27 May 1828
WATSON, Ebenezer	SIMONDS, Mary 1st, Rev. James Welch	MOG 3 May 1820
WATSON, Samuel R. all of Bonhomme, St. Louis Co. 18th inst, Gabriel Long, Esq.	THOMPSON, Ann	MOG 27 Jan. 1816
WEATHERBIE, F. J.	BLACKBURN, Jane E. at Vine Cottage, Joliet, IL n.d., Rev. Briggs	MORE 12 Aug. 1850
WEEKS, Solomon	BOWEN, Ann Maria (Richard) 2nd, Squire Mack	WEM 13 June 1839
WEIRICK, R. C. of New Orleans	SCUDDER, Mary E. (Charles) of St. Louis 29 June, Elder Joseph Challon of Cincinnati	MORE 7 July 1847
WELLS, Jno. W.	PRICE, Martha A. 8th, Rev. Kemp Scott	JEFRE 10 May 1834
WELLS, John	TAYLOR, Harriet of Philadelphia 8th inst., Hinton	MORE 10 June 1843
WELLS, Peter	JOHNSON, Elizabeth 14 Aug., Philip Cassily, Esq.	COMB 17 Aug. 1836
WELLS, Wm. H. of Newburyport, Mass.	GRAVES, Lydia S. of St. Louis, at Niagara Falls 30th ult.	MORE 10 Aug. 1849
WELSH, George S. of St. Louis	TUFTS, Lucy of and at New Orleans 16th, Rev. Wm. Curtis	MORE 27 Jan. 1844

85

WENDOVER, Joseph R.   LUYSTER, Mary Ann (A.R., Esq.)   MORE
of St. Louis   at Trinity Church, NY   20 Sept. 1850
                             17 Sept.

WESTERMAN, Henry   BURG, Margaret   MORE
                             1 Jan., J. W. Walsh, JP   9 Jan. 1838

WETMORE, Leoniadas   D'BOUIS, Amelia Catherine Sophia MORE
                             of Mexico, at New Orleans   28 March 1849
                             14th inst., Rev. Fr. Mane

WETMORE, Thaddeus E., Esq.   CONGER, Carolinue U.   MORE
of St. Louis   of and at Galesburg, IL   25 April 1850
                             11 April, by Rev. Blanchard,
                             Pres. Knox College

WHALEY, William   WYMER, Mrs. Rebecca   PWH
                            14 March, Jacob Creath, Jr.   18 March 1843

WHEATON, Edward S.   FINNEY, Jane A. (eld., Wm.) ,   SWERE
                            28 Oct., Rev. Boyle   1 Nov. 1847

WHEELER, Capt. Amos   CHARLESS, Ann (Joseph)   SCMO
                            at St. Louis   6 June 1822
                            1st, R. Peck

WHERRY, Daniel Boone   WEST, Clarissa   MORE
                            Gasconade Co., 20th ult.   3 April 1832

WHERRY, Joseph A.   HARNER, Amelia Harriet   COMB
of St. Louis   (Col. W.B.R.) of and at.   16 Nov. 1835
                            Helena, Ark. Terr.
                            5 Nov., Judge Lacy

WHITE, George   WELLS, Miss _____   MORE
of Bonhomme, St. L. Co.   of Gravois, St. L. Co.   15 Feb. 1831
                            Thurs., Rev. John Brown

WHITE, George W.   CHILTON, Mary   JINQ
                            19 Sept., Rev. Morris   30 Oct. 1844

WHITE, Henry   DINES, Martha W.   PWH
                            in Shelby Co.   9 Dec. 1847
                            25 Nov., Rev. Sigler

WHITE, Thomas S.   COLE, Mary C. (Capt. G. B.)   MORE
both of Washington Co.   n.d., Rev. A. H. Rogers   31 Oct. 1849
                            of Farmington

WHITE, W. W.   ATHERTON, Frances A.   MORE
of St. Louis   of NY, at Jacksonville   18 April 1846
                            14th inst., Rev. Wm. Williams

WHITE, William   TOOLEY, Mary   MIN
both of Chariton Co.   20 May, Eb. Rodgers   29 May 1824

WHITE, William H.   KEITH, Ellen M.   MORE
                           formerly Rochester, NY   27 Jan. 1842
                           24 Jan., Rev. Peake, Christ Church

WHITLOCK, Andrew S.   O'HARA, Margaret A.   MORE
of Louisville (?)   of St. Louis, at Louisville   15 Nov. 1838
                           n.d., Rev. S. P. Humphrey

WICKLIFFE, Capt. Wm. N.   HERTZOG, Ann   MORE
                           at Cantonment Leavenworth   20 Dec. 1831
                           14th ult.

WICKS, George H., Esq.   CRIPPEN, Mary Ann   SWERE
of Philadelphia   7 Oct., Rev. Childs   11 Oct. 1847

WIDENER, Ludwig,   AKER, Barbara   MORE
                           formerly of Bavaria   10 Dec. 1850
                           9 Dec., McKenney, JP

WIER, George   Lalamiere, Susan M.   MORE
of St. Louis   of and at Kaskaskia   14 March 1848
                           24 Feb., Rev. Fahey

WILCOX, Seymour B.   MACKLIF, Julia F.   MORE
                           4 Aug., Winwright, JP   8 Oct. 1848

WILKINSON, Nathaniel   FRANCIS, Rebecca   MORE
                           5 Dec., Rev. Lee   10 Dec. 1848

WILKINSON, Thos. P.   CABELL, Jane B.   BOLT
all of Chariton Co.   27th, Rev. W. G. Caples   13 Dec. 1845

WILLIAMS, Marcus   CLARK, Susannah H. (Bennet)   MIN
of Cooper Co.   8th inst.   12 March 1821

WILLIAMS, Powell   GRAGG, Sarah   MIN
                           29 Jan., N. S. Burckhartt, Esq.   6 Feb. 1829

WILLIAMS, Samuel R.   MARS, Almira Jane   MORE
of Henry Co.   of Johnson Co.   1 Jan. 1849
                           13th, Rev. Wm. Caldwell

WILLIAMSON, James   HODGE, Helen (Josiah)   JINQ
                           n.d., no minister   25 Dec. 1841

WILLIS, Charles   CHANDLER, Matilda (Oliver)   MORE
of Willis & Stevens,   at Boston   6 Oct. 1837
St. Louis   20th ult., Rev. Stow

WILLSON, Robert   LEAR, Lavina   PWH
all of Shelby Co.   28 Jan., Henry Louthan   4 Feb. 1847

WILSON, ___thion (see Wilson, Zion)	GREEN, Sarah Elizabeth 18th inst., Thomas, JP	MORE 6 March 1843
WILSON, John, Esq. attorney	PULLIAM, Ann R. (Drury, Esq.) in Saline Co., 27 Nov.	MIN 2 Dec. 1825
WILSON, John B. formerly NY	HEMPSTEAD, Cornelia V. (late Thomas) 26th, Bishop Hawks	MORE 28 Oct. 1848
WILSON, John C.	ALLEN, Joanna (Judson) at St. Paul's Church 13 Feb., Bishop Hawks	SWERE 21 Feb. 1848
WILSON, Pliny all of Howard Co.	TODD, Spicy 10th inst., Elder C. E. Russell	BOLT 13 May 1843
WILSON, Zion	GREEN, Sarah Eliza 4th inst., L. B. Thomas, JP	OSD 7 March 1843
WILT, Christian	WILSON, Ann (Major George) 10th	MOG 21 Jan. 1815
WINDSOR, H. H.	HICKMAN, Caroline (ygst., late Dr. David of Wooster, Ohio) 4 May, Hinton	MORE 8 May 1843
WINN, James	PARKS, Rebecca near Chariton 30 April, Eb. Rodgers	MIN 20 May 1823
WINN, John of Rochester, NY	JAYNES, Matilda 9 Aug., Rev. Jacob Taylor	MORE 11 Aug. 1849
WINSOR, Wm. T. of Lexington, MO	CARPENTER, Mary (Judge) at Bardstown, KY 11th, Rev. Crosby	MORE 17 Oct. 1848
WINSTON, Thomas, merchant of Jefferson City,	MILLER, Sally C. 19 Dec.	BRUNS 30 Dec. 1848
WITHNELL, John	WAINWRIGHT, Martha G. (Joseph of Winterton Brewery near Lawrenceville in Allegheny Co.) in Pittsburgh, n.d. Rev. John Taylor	FREEP 28 Feb. 1833
WOLFE, J. B.	THOMSON, Elizabeth of Charleston, S.C., at St. George's Church 10 Sept., Rev. Horrell	SWERE 17 Sept. 1848
WOOD, David	(?)KAYLOR, S.C. at house of John K. Taylor Shelby Co., 12th Rev. S. C. McConnell	PWH 25 Feb. 1843

WOOD, Dr. John S.   BUCKNER, M. E. (Samuel, Esq.)   LEXP
of Lexington   of and at Jackson Co.   6 May 1845
                           20 April, Rev. J. L. Yantis

WOOD, Thomas   GRICE, Margaret S.   MORE
both of St. Louis   in Belleville, IL   1 Aug. 1850
                           28 July, Rev. Ramsay

WOOD, William A.   HODGMAN, Marie   MORE
                           late of St. Louis, at Quincy, IL 3 Dec. 1840
                           Thurs. eve. last

WOODRUFF, Marcus P., Esq. BRANT, Mary W. (Randolph, Esq.) MORE
both of St. Louis   in New York, 22 July   3 Aug. 1847

WOODS, James B.   GOOD, Martha A. (Maj. John A.) GLWT
first clerk of steamboat   at Buffalo Knob   9 Dec. 1852
Martha Jewett   18th ult (from Pike Co. Record)

WOODS, John C.   HASTEN, Ann Eliza   BRUNS
all of Howard Co.   Wed. last   2 March 1848

WOODSON, Samuel   BATES, Maria (Elias)   MORE
                           at Herculaneum, 27th inst.   3 July 1822

WOODWARD, Edward K.   SIZER, Mary   MORE
                           3rd inst., I. T. Hinton   5 Jan. 1834

WOODWORTH, A. L.   WETHERILL, Margaret H. (W.H.)   MORE
of Peru, NY   of St. Louis, at res. of   30 Dec. 1843
                           R. W. Poindexter, Allegheny City
                           7th inst., Rev. Dunlap

WOOLDRIDGE, Tilden W.   SQUIRE, Julia (Judge Samuel)   MORE
                           at res. her father, Madison Co., IL 2 Feb. 1850
                           27 Jan.

WOOLLEY, Col. A. R.   PRESTON, Caroline L. (late   MORE
U. S. Army   Maj. Wm.) at Louisville,KY   27 Sept. 1827
                           13th

WORKMAN, David   HOOK, Nancy   MIN
Both of this place   at New Franklin   18 Dec. 1829
                           8 Dec., Rev. H. Chamberlain

WORLEY, Charles Woodruff   SANDFORD, Catawea   MORE
midshipman, U.S.N.   of St. Louis, at Louisville, KY 17 Oct. 1848
                           18th inst., St. Paul's Church

WORTHINGTON, Elijah R.   BACON, Sarah L. (L.)   MOG
merchant of Chesterfield   of this county   8 March 1820
                           Sunday last, Rev. James Craig

WRIGHT, Elder Allen of Christian Church	FRISTOE, Lydia V. (Amos) of Georgetown, MO at Jefferson City, 22nd ult	MODE 6 Jan. 1847
WRIGHT, Hon. F. B.	McLANAHAN, Nancy J. at Scott Co. 29th ult, Rev. Jackson	MORE 15 Sept. 1837
WRIGHT, Henry C.	MARTIN, Frances Ann in Montgomery Co. 2_th inst, Rev. George Clay	MORE 13 March 1832
YATES, John D.	ROBINSON, Mrs. Eliza at res. Mrs. Comfort Wright 15 Oct., Rev. Boyle	MORE 16 Oct. 1850
YOUNG, John L. of St. Louis	WILCOX, Julia L. (John) of and at New Orleans 1 Aug., Rev. Clapp	MORE 10 Aug. 1842
YOUNG, Nelson A. formerly of St. Louis	WILCOX, Caroline of and at New Orleans 16th inst., Rev. Joel Parker	MORE 30 April 1838
YOUNG, Robert	HALFORD, Lucinda of Madison Co., IL 17 Aug., Wilson Primm, Esq.	SCOMB 19 Aug. 1835
YOUNG, William attorney	BOYD, Martha Ann (Col. G.) of Shelby Co., KY (and at?) 11th inst., Rev. Shannon	MORE 23 Aug. 1831
YOUNGER, Charles of Clay Co.	TAYLOR, Amelia of Franklin 14th, Justinian Williams	MIN 4 Dec. 1824
YOUNT, Capt. Geo.	NEWMAN, Margaret C. (Michael) in 2nd Presbyterian Church 21st, Rev. Goodrich	MORE 26 Nov. 1848
ZAFF, Godfred of Hannibal	SPRANGLEY, Harriet of Palmyra, in Quincy n.d.	PWH 23 Oct. 1845

INDEX TO BRIDES

ABEL, Elizabeth - HANLEY, Francis
ABEL, Susan - ELDER, Lewis P.
ABRAMS, Ann Eliza - FOSTER, Abial W.
ACHLAND, Sarah Ann - SHEPARD, John B.
ACKLEY, Hannah - RANDALL, John D.
ADDISON, Anna Maria - SAVAGE, Wm. H.
AESONACGLE, Paulina - JARRETT, E. M.
AINSLIE, Mrs. Mary - HOGAN, John S. C.
AKER, Barbara - WIDENER, Ludwig
ALBRIGHT, Catharine - MARTIN, James
ALDRICH, Louisa M. - COOLY, Martin
ALEXANDER, Apolline - BLAIR, Francis P.
ALEXANDER, (Rebecca) Harriet -
  BATES, Thomas (Lothrop)
ALEXANDER, Mrs. Theresa (nee Pratte) -
  PEUGNET, Lewis D.
ALLEGA, Talitha - STREET, Geo. W.
ALLEN, Elizabeth A. - EWING, E. B.
ALLEN, Joanna - WILSON, John C.
ALLEN, Sarah A. - GERARD, William
ALLINGTON, Mary - BRIGGS, Thomas
ALLISON, Statyra - CRISSWELL, George
ANDREWS, Sarah Ann - ANDREWS, James L.
ANDREWS, Sarah F. - MAURICE, W. H.
ANTHONY, Henrietta B. - LADD, James S.
ARMSTRONG, Eliza - MUIR, Wm. E.
ARMSTRONG, Mary Ann - PEYRAU, Feaben
ARRAT, Barbara - KESSELRING, Adam
ARREN, Soledad - LEITENSDORFER, Dr.
  Eugene
ATCHISON, Elizabeth - THOMAS, Ezra
ATHERTON, Frances A. - WHITE, W. W.
ATKINS, Emily - PETTES, Eleazer P.
ATKINSON, Mary - STEUART, A.D.
AULD, Zipporah W. - THATCH, T. H.
AULL, Lavinia - DAY, Franklin O.
AUSTIN, Mary S. - HONEY, John W.
AYRES, Emily - STEWART, Dr. A.
AYRES, Rebeckah A. - PARMER, Anthony C.

BACON, Elvira M. - FERGERSON, Thos. J.
BACON, Sarah L. - WORTHINGTON,
  Elijah R.
BAILEY, Mrs. Atalanta - POWERS, Wm.
BAILEY, Mrs. Margaret A. - RISLY or
  RUBY, David R.
BAILEY, Mary (widow) - CROPPER, Levin
BAILEY, Mary L. - BROWN, Thomas

BAILEY, Sabra Caroline - PEART,
  Boanerges E.
BAIRD, Mrs. Mary - PROCTOR, Dr. W.H.
BAKER, Artimisa J. - HEADLEY, Rev.
  J. H.
BAKER, Susan - SMITH, J. Perrine
BALDWIN, Anna Theresa - PHILLIPS,
  Robert B.
BALL, Mary C. - GAREY, Henry F.
BALLARD, Mrs. Mary - CUNIFFE, John B.
BANKS, Louisa Ann - HULL, William C.
BARGER, Amelia - CRAIG, John
BARNES, Sophia - BOGGS, Thomas J.
BARNES, Mrs. Eliza - HEMPSTEAD,
  Charles S.
BARNES, Susan H.- MATTHEWS, John
BARNETT, Mary E. - MILAN, J. C.
BARR, Sarah - DRYDEN, John D.S.
BARTHALOW, Ann E. - SMITH, I. T.
BARTLETT, Susan Walker - FARWELL,
  Abel G.
BARTLETT, Thomasella - SHORTRIDGE,
  Dr. William T.
BARTON, Eliza - BENOIS, Louis
BASYE, Elizabeth - HOLLIDAY, Benjamin
BASEY, Louisa - MILLER, George W.
BATES, Adaline - LEWIS, Samuel W.
BATES, Ann Eliza - MORRIS, S. A.
BATES, Maria - WOODSON, Samuel
BATES, _____ - HONEY, J. W.
BAXTER, Lydia - BROWN, William
BAYLEY, Mrs. Julia E. - CAPLES,
  Rev. W. G.
BEALL, Ellen - CAUGHLIN, David
BECKWITH, Caroline - WALES, Dexter T.
BEEBE, Sarah A. - STAHL, Nicholas
BEEDING, America - SUMMERS, Maston T.
BELL, Margaret D. - BLAINE, John L.
BELL, Martha M. - BLUE, Dr. John M.
BELL, Sarah Ann - COLLIER, George
BELT, Sarah E. - CARROLL, Charles C.
BELT, Sarah Jane V. - BARRON, Thos. M.
BELTZHOOVER, Elizabeth - COX, Wm.
BENJAMIN, Malinda M. - ILLES, Elijah
BENJAMIN, Sarah - DuBOIS, C.
BENNETT, Cecile - JONES, George
BENNETT, Jessie - HOOD, Robert
BENNETT, Mrs. Margaret Ann -
  HOLDERNESS, William

BENNETT, Patience - HENRY, Isaac
BENSVILLE, Mme. Celine D. - OUDARD,
    Louis
BENT, Dorcas - CARR, Wm. C.
BENT, Julia Ann - BOGGS, Lilburn W.
BENTON, Mary T. - BRIGGS, Ebenezer
BENTON, Eliza Preston Carrington -
    JONES, Wm. Carey
BERKLEY, Ann Elizabeth - POSTON,
    Milton
BERRY, Sarah Jane - ENNIS, Wm.
BICKMORE, Anna - PETTINGILL, Daniel
BIGELOW, Mary - HOOPER, Clark
BILLENS, Sarah Ann - LESH, Andrew
BILLON, Emily - ATCHISON, John
BILLON, Virginia - GRATIOT, Paul
BIRD, Joanna L. - BREED, Aaron E.
BIRON, Eliza - CHRISTMAN, Wm.
BISHOP, Harriet - VAN DEVANTER, Wm.
BISSELL, Cornelia R. - DOUGLASS,
    Thompson
BISSELL, Mary - PRICE, Risdon H.
BLACKBURN, Georgianna - DOSSETT,
    Henry L.
BLACKBURN, Jane E. - WEATHERBIE, F. J.
BLACKISTON, Martha W. - KNEEDLER,
    Jacob
BLAIR, Eliza - LANGHAM, Elias T.
BLEDSOE, Emily E. - HEATON, Dr. O.R.
BLESSING, Susan - EIDSON, Newton
BLOCK, Delia - BLOCK, Phinehas
BLOY, Louisa - BOON, Hampton L.
BOLLING, Harriet - HALSEY, William
BOOKER, Henrietta Maria - PRATHER,
    J. V.
BOON, Ann Eliza - HURD (HEARD), Wm. T.
BOONE, Delinda - CRAIG, Rev. James
BOONE, Harriett M. - BABER, Hiram H.
BOONE, Jane A. - LOWRY, E. P.
BOONE, Melcina - SMITH, James C.
BOONE, Pantha - BOGGS, Lilburn W.
BOSS, Mary Ann L. - AUSTIN, Wm. James
BOSSERON, Susan - FARNHAM, Russell
BOSWELL, Jane - SINGLE, Benjamin
BOURN, Mrs. Christian - LONGMIRE, Wm.
BOUTON, Sarah A. - HEMPSTEAD, Wm.
BOWEN, Ann Maria - WEEKS, Solomon
BOWEN, Eliza Seymore - FARRIS, Robert P.
BOWEN, Susan Amanda - HUGHES, Richard C.
BOYCE, Ann T. - GERARD (JARRED), Wm.
BOYCE, Margaret - ROE, Joseph

BOYCE, Martha Ann - KENNETT, L. M.
BOYD, Martha Ann - YOUNG, William
BOZARTH, Elenora - VICOREY, Francis M.
BRADFORD, Virginia - BLANCHARD, Benj.
BRADY, Mrs.___ - LILLEY (RILEY?), John
BRANNIN, Elizabeth - SCOTT, lewis
BRANT, Mary W. - WOODRUFF, Marcus P.
BRAZEAU,____ - SANGUINETTE, Chas., Jr.
BREED, Lydia Maria - ABBOTT, John C.
BREVARD, Margaret - PRIESTLY, Dr.___
BRIGGS, Mrs. Kate - SELLS, Walter
BRITTINGHAM, Sarah M. - HICKMAN,
    Capt. P. A.
BRITTON, Emma L. - SHANNON, A. J.
BRODE, Margaret - HENRY, Thomas
BROOKHART, Ann Cecelia - CARTER, John F.
BROOKS, Angeline - HORN, Dr. Wm. T.
BROWN, Christina - ENGELS, Nathaniel
BROWN, Ellen - CHILDS, Benj. Frank.
BROWN, Harriet - JOHNSON, James
BROWN, Lucia Emelie - BROWNELL,
    Isaac W.
BROWN, Margaret Ann - JONES, Russell
BROWN, Mary Fletcher - COCK, Wm. M.
BROWN, Nancy Agnes - NEILL, Andrew
BROWNER, Cynthia A. - RICHARDS, B.S.
BRUMBAUGH, Mary - MURRAY, Joseph
BUCKNER, M. E. - WOOD, Dr. John S.
BUFORD, Elizabeth Gabriella -
    RYLAND, John F.
BUFORD, Emily - HUMPHREY, Thomas
BURBANKS, Elizabeth - BANNEN, Horace
BURCKHARTT, Mary Ann - REDMAN, Rev.
    Wm. Winn
BURK, Elizabeth W. - PATTERSON, Joseph
BURK, Mary Ann - MITCHELL, Leonard
BURG, Margaret - WESTERMAN, Henry
BURNS, Mary Ann - McGUIRE, John
BURT, Jane J. - SHURLDS, Henry
BUTTS, Ellen - JAMES, Levi

CABANNE, Julia - KINGSBURY, James W.
CABELL, Jane B. - WILKINSON, Thos. P.
CALDWELL, Sarah - BARR, Forrister
CALHOUN, Harriet A. - HOLLIDAY, Dr.
    Charles H.
CALLAHAN, Mary Jane - ALLABAUGH, John R.
CALLOT, Judith - OBUCHON, Francis
CALWAY, Frances E. - MARTIEN, Dr.
    James M.
CAMPBELL, Mary E. - TAYLOR, John H.

CAMPBELL, Sarah - TAYLOR, Thomas
CANTER, Edith - TAYLOR, Johnson
CANTON, Eliza - DWYER, William J.
CARLDON, Angeline - RIDER, Samuel
CARNS, Adelaide G. - TOWNSEND, James
CARPENTER, Mary - WINSOR, Wm. T.
CARR, Mrs. Elizabeth - CHAMBERS, A.B.
CARROLL, Katherine - BYRNE, Michael
CARROLL, Mary - GREEN, William B.
CARROLL, Mary C. - JOHNSON, G. Edward
CARSON, Martha Jane - CLUFF, Samuel
CARTMILL, Mrs. Maria - DUNLAVY,
   Richard
CASE, Beulah Ann H. - KIRKPATRICK, Wm.
CASE, Catharine - NELSON, Wm. S.
CASE, Louisa M. - SPENCER, John W.
CASKIE, Nannie J. - HARRISON, Saml. J.
CASON, Ann E. - BURRISS, Davenport
CASON, Martha E. - HYATT, Joseph L.
CATON, Mary - TOMPKINS, George
CERE, Mary - COPES, Thomas P.
CHALLACOMB, Isabella - HEDENBERG,
   John
CHAMBERLAIN, Julia F. - LEDFORD, Wm.H.
CHAMBERLAIN, Mary - EDWARDS, Joseph
CHANDLER, Matilda - WILLIS, Charles
CHANE, Martha - GRAHAM, Alexander
CHAPEL, Mrs. Ella A. - HOPSON,
   Winthrop
CHAPMAN, Eliza R. - FOLEY, J.
CHAPMAN, Fanny Folger - THORNBURG,
   William A.
CHARLESS, Ann - WHEELER, Amos
CHARLEVILLE, Miss ___ - BATTU, Mr.__
CHASE, Chloe Marie - AKENS, John Lewis
CHAUNCEY, Emily - HAYES, Benj.
CHENIE, Rene Marie Julie - GOURD,
   L. Henry
CHILD, Sarah J. - GOODRICH, James C.
CHILDS, Ellen Ann - CLARK, Henry
CHILTON, Mary - WHITE, George W.
CHOTEAU, Marie Louise - PAUL, Gabriel
CHOUQUETTE, Eulalie - COURTOIS, Joseph
CHOUTEAU, Miss ___ - PAUL, Dr.
CHOUTEAU, Julia - MAFFITT, William
CHRISMAN, Mrs. Catherine - VIVION,
   Flavel
CHRISTY, Eliza - ASHLEY, William
CHRISTY, Harriet - DEAN, James
CLAPP, Georgianna Wingate - RAY,
   Winthrop G.
CLARK, Anne E. - BROWN, Livingston
CLARK, Gwinthlean - MACRAE, N.C.
CLARK, Harriet B. - MARVIN, Enoch M.

CLARK, Jane - BALL, John M.
CLARK, Lucy L. - DAWSON, John
CLARK, Sue - TOMPKINS, Benj.
CLARK, Susan - HOLMAN, Richard
CLARK, Susannah H. - WILLIAMS, Marcus
CLEARY, Mrs. Ann - COSGREAVE, Moses
CLENDENIN, Minnie - COURTENAY, Thomas E.
CLINETINCH, Matulda - PAYTON, John S.
CLINKINBEARD, Mary L. - BARTLETT,
   Joseph
CLOY, Rosina Ann - TEMPLAR, Louis
COCK, Lucy A. - BRENKER, Isaac
COCKRELL, Emeline - FLOYD, David
COGSWELL, Fanny - MATTHEWS, James P.
COLE, Mary C. - WHITE, Thomas S.
COLEMAN, Mary Ann - MORRISON, Wm. V.
COLLET, Emma S. - TAYLOR, Thomas M.
COLLIER, Mrs.Diana - ANDERSON, Stephen
COLLINGWORTH, Martha - JOHNSON,
   Ambrose
COLLINS, Isaetta - BARTON, K. L.
COLLINS, Martha L. - CONWAY, F. R.
CONGER, Caroline U. - WETMORE,
   Thaddeus E.
CONKLIN, Maria A. - ANGNEY, W. Z.
CONSTANT, Julia Ann - RINGER,
   Matthias P.
CONSTANT, Julia A. Francis - KENNEDY,
   Robert P.
CONWAY, Ann - POLLOCK, James
CONWAY, Sarah - SHEPPARD, Joseph M.
CONWAY, Sarah - SHEPHERD, Jas. M.
COOK, Mrs. Huldah - BORTON, John
COOK, Louisa M. - FITCH, McConal
COOK, Sarah J. - TAYLOR, Thomas J.
COOK, Susan - MORAN, Francis
COOLY, Lucinda - DUNKLIN, James
COOPER, Amanda - McREYNOLDS, Allen
COOPER, Harriet J. - EDWARDS, Nelson G.
COOPER, Mary - KAVANAUGH, Charles M.
COOPER, Sallie H. - CARTER, Rinaldo S.
COPHER, Sarah - CORNELIUS, James
CORD, Amelia - VIZZELL, Jacob
CORDELL, Amelia C. - NEWTON, Thos. W.
CORDELL, Missouri Ann - STEVENS, R.H.
CORDELL, Polly - LANHAM, Stephen
CORWITH, Phoebe R. - REILLY, Robt. A.
COULTER, Caroline J. - GAMBLE,
   Hamilton R.
COURTNEY, Sarah - VAN BIBBER, Ewing
COWEN, Henrietta Frances - SPRATT,
   G. W.
COZZENS, Catherine - GOULD, Wm.
CRANCH, Abby Adams - ELLIOT, Rev. Wm.
   G.   93

CRAWLEY, Elizabeth Ann - DAVIS,
 Henry H.
CREASON, Mary - TEETER, Gerrard
CRESAP, Isabella Jane - GARLAND, B.S.
CRIPPIN, Mary Ann - WICKS, Geo. H.
CRITTENDEN, Kate - HOYLE, George
CROMWELL, Mary - DEWITT, A. B.
CROSS, Mary Josephine - SHAW, Thos.
CROWELL, Eunice - HALLET, Moses
CUBBERLY, Mrs. Maria C. - HARRISON,
 Enos H.
CULVER, Miss ___ - FORSYTHE, Robt.
CUMMINGS, Martha A. - MAXWELL, Henry
CUMMINS, Elizabeth - REPPY, Henry G.
CUMMINS, Letitia - SAMUEL, Giles M.
CUNNINGHAM, Mrs. Caroline - JOHNSON,
 Andrew
CUNNINGHAM, Caroline - DUGAN, Robert
CUNNINGHAM, Francis - KUYKENDALL,
 Jacob

DAGGETT, Harriet H. - STAGG, Edward
DAMERON, Martha - SMITH, Robert
DANIELS, Catherine - MAWDESLEY,
 Richard
DANIELS, Mary E. - DRUILLARD, Louis
DAVENPORT, Almira A. - HAWKS, Geo. M.
DAVENPORT, Margaret M. - FETTE, H.G.
DAVENPORT, Mary - CLAFLIN, William
DAVID, Caroline B. - MAXWELL, Henry
DAVIDSON, Frances - RUSSELL, John B.
DAVIS, Abby Low - THOMPSON, Wildes T.
DAVIS, Mrs. Jane F. - HOLLINGSHEAD,
 John S.
DAVIS, Mary Lewis - ROGERS, Joseph P.
DAVIS, Nancy - McARDLE, James
DAYS, Polly Ann - RENALS, William
D'BOUIS, Amelia Cath. Sophia -
 WETMORE, Leoniadas
DEAN, Eliza A. - FAYERWEATHER, James
DEANE, Jennie - HOSKINS, Charles
DEAUGHERTY, Mrs. Elizabeth - SHARP,
 William
DEAVER, Elizabeth - RAGSDALE, Richard
DEFOREST, Ellen Jane - DEAN, Geo. B.
DE HAAN, Anney -EMANUEL, Isaac
DE HAAN, Catherine - LICHTENSTEIN,
 Solomon H.
DE LA TOUR, Julia A. - McLAUGHLIN,
 John
DELAURIERE, Clarisse Ozite F. - DUVAL,
 Richard M.
DeLAURIER, Susan C. A. F. - BRIGHT,
 George Y.

DEMPSTER, Adelina - BLUNT, Charles
DePREFONTAINE, Mary Ann - LLOYD,
 James F.
DICKINSON, Frances R. - LYMAN, James
DILLER, Sarah E. - THOMPSON, James P.
DILLON, Susan F. - STEVENS, Chas. W.
DIMMITT, Catharine G. - BUFORD, Merry
DINES, Martha W. - WHITE, Henry
DOAK, Lavinia D. - HOLLAND, Richard E.
DODSON, P. C. - HARRISON, B. B.
DOUGLASS, Eliza - PAGE, Wm.
DOYLE, Lucinda Julia Ann - HUDSON,
 John H.
DRAGOON, Temperance - MATTOX, Thos.
DRAKE, Mary Jane - HEDDY, James
DREW, Mary - BEACH, Milan
DREW, Sarah - SPARR, ___
DRURY, Mrs. Mary - HORINE, M. F.
DuBOIS, Josephine - BENOIST, S.H.
DuBREUIL, Constance - CHOUTEAU, Paul L.
DUDLEY, Ann Virginia - BROADDUS,
 W. H. C.
DUFF, Lucinda - HUMPHREY, David
DUFFEY, Louisa M. - EMERSON, John S.
DUGAN, Mary Ann - FURGESON, Jonas
DUNCAN, Miss ___ - LYNN, Wm.
DUNCAN, Mary - SHAW, Robert
DUNKLIN, Eliza Lucinda - McGREADY,
 Wm. Edward
DUNN, Eliza - McENNIS, Michael
DUNN, Mary A. - MULLTEN, T.
DUNNICA, America V. - CUTRER, Isaac W.
DURNO, Margaret - SHEPHERDSON, Jno. K.
DUSTON, Elazema - BALDWIN, Robert

EACHES, Mary - BLACKISTON, Nathaniel
EADS, Eliza Jane - DILLON, P. M.
EADS, Polly - CAMP, Hiram
EASTON, Mary - SIBLEY, George C.
EASTON, Joanna A. - QUARLES, Pryor
EDDY, Ann Amelia - BISHOP, Martin W.
EDGAR, Mrs. M. Eliza - PASCHALL, N.
EDMONSTON, Angeline - LICKLIDER,
 Solomon Lewis
EDWARDS, Julia - COOK, Daniel P.
EDWARDS, Lucretia - FRENCH, Parker
EDWARDS, Miranda B. - SEBREE, Laban
ELIOT, Caroline - KASSON, John A.
ELLINGTON, Mrs. E. - SOUTHERLAND,
 George
ELLIOT, Eliza Ann - HENDERSON, Joseph
ELLIOT, Mrs. Mary - SPENCER, M. C.
ELLIOT, Mary Lewis - DELASSUS, Lnon

94

ELLIS, Mary - PEMBERTON, John
ELSTON, Eliza - HILL, Madison
EMBRY, Mrs. Sarah - CHISM, Howard
ENGLISH, Patsy - CONSTER, George
ESSEX, Eleanor - MITCHELL, Edward
EVANS, Harriet D. - SETTLE, Wm. H.
EVERHEART, Susanah - HESSER, F.
EWING, Pamelia - READ, J. W.

FALWELL, Elizabeth Ann - MARTIN,
  John M.
FAREWELL, Louisa - BERRY, Henry B.
FARIS, Catherine - CLINTON, Charles D.
FAY, Ellen Maria - MACUBIN, Charles N.
FENNINGTON, Hesta - DALY, John
FERGUSON, Eliza - KINGSLAND, George
FICKLIN, Frances Marshall - COONS, A.J.
FIELDS, Caroline B. - SMARR, Abner
FINNEY, Jane A. - WHEATON, Edward S.
FISH, Jane Maria - EAGER, John M.
FISHER, Cornelia - BELL, Joseph
FISHER, Eliza - HAYS, Orin
FISHBACK, Frances Ann - GRAHAM, Robt.
FISHER, Jemima - ANDERSON, G. A.
FISHER, Mary Elizabeth - HOMER,
  Thomas J.
FLEISCHMAN, Henrietta A. - COLE,
  David V.
FLEMING, Honora - HARRINGTON, Jeremiah
FLEMMINGS, Eliza - KIVETT, Madison
FOOT, Caroline - RISLEY, Luke
FORD, Ann - SEXTON, James
FORD, Jane - CARTER, Eli
FORDER, Sarah Anna - BURNETT,
  George, Jr.
FORGVERAN, Clemency P. - BOURN, Reuben
FOSTER, Clarissa - JENNINGS, Wm.
FOSTER, H. B. - CROSMAN, G. H.
FOUCHE, Louisa - KELLAM, Chas. D.
FOULKE, Minerva - ORR, William
FOURT, Margaret - BUTLER, John
FRANCIS, Rebecca - WILKINSON, Nathaniel
FRANCISCO, Mary M. - HARRIS, W. W.
FRAY, Catherine - FENWICK, Lewis
FREEMAN, Nancy - VANLANDINGHAM,
  Samuel
FRENY, Mrs. Anastasia - WALSH, James
FRISTOE, Elizabeth - TABOR, E. A.
FRISTOE, Lydia V. - WRIGHT, Allen
FULBACK, Mrs. Rosanna - MANNING,
  Michael

GAITHER, Matilda - PATTEN, Nathaniel
GALASPE, Ellen Ann - TAYLOR, John Holmes
GALBRETH, Martha - COOPER, Benjamin
GALLISON, Charlotte G. - HOLDEN,
  Edward
GANDLEY, Eliza A. - GARRITY, James
GANTT, Elenora - NELSON, Arthur
GANTT, Mary - GUEST, Jonathon
GARDINER, Melani Veron - STEWART,
  Thomas J.
GARDNER, Elizabeth - CRAWFORD, David
GARNER, Elizabeth E. - SAMUEL, Edward M.
GARY, Rachel - FINCH, William M.
GAULDING, Mary - DAVIS, Robert T.
GAW, Elizabeth - SCOTT, James
GAW, Jane - MELODY, George H. C.
GENTRY, Martha - BURRESS, Samuel
GERS, Helena Maria - HEISLEN, Aloys
GEYER, Harriet - NORRIS, James
GIBBS, Abbey F. - LINDSLEY, J. C.
GILBRETH, Jane G. - MEGAFFIGAN, Peter
GILLESPIE, Caroline - HALLAM, Alexander
GILMAN, Prudence - LACKAY, Hugh
GIVENS, Sarah F. - PATTEN, Thos. W.
GLASBY, Ruth Anna - McCUNE, John S.
GLASGOW, M. S. - CLARK, J. K.
GLEM, Emma J. - AMOS, W. W.
GODAIR, Elizabeth -LIGHTNER, L. S.
GODFREY, Mary - HENDERSON, George
GODMAN, Nancy - McCOLLOUGH, Andrew
GOOCH, Mary Jane - FOSTER, Richard
GOOD, Martha A. - WOODS, James B.
GOODFELLOW, Eliza Ann - BURD, John W.
GOODING, Mrs. Lucy - JOHNSON, J. W.
GOODING, Mary Jane - CUNNINGHAM, Jos.
GOODRICH, E. A. - SCOTT, Charles M.
GORDON, Maria - GIBSON, William
GORDON, Sarah - RICE, Wm. R.
GORMON, Mary Jane - THROCKMORTON, J.
GOWDY, Anna - McCAMPBELL, Thomas C.
GRAGG, Sarah - WILLIAMS, Powell
GRATIOT, Emile - CHOUTEAU, Peter, Jr.
GRATIOT, Isabelle - DeMUN, M. ___
GRATTON, Margaretta - PERRY, R. P.
GRAVES, Lydia - WELLS, Wm. H.
GREATHOUSE, Eliza Jane - PURKY, P. M.
GREEN, Adeliza - HUNT, John F.
GREEN, Julia Ann - GREGORY, George H.
GREEN, Sarah Elizabeth - WILSON, Zion
  (or ____thion)
GREEN, Susan - SAMUEL, Thomas J.
GREGG, Mary - BAYFIELD, James H.
GREGOIRE, Mary - ST. VRAIN, Felix
GRICE, Margaret S. - WOOD, Thomas

GRIERSON, Margaret - PHILIPS, Thomas C.
GRIFFIN, Deborah H. - HESTON, Henry J.
GRIFFITH, Polly - CLELAND, Beriah
GRIMAU, Virginia - BEAUFILS, Joseph
GROGAN, Rhoda - LEER, Henry P.
GRUN, Mary - GAVIN, William
GRUNDY, Miss ___ - BASS, John M.
GRUTTER, Elizabeth - HUNE, Edward
GUERNSEY, Frances J. - HARLOW, Wm. M.
GUITARD, Julia - MONTAIGNE, Joseph, Jr.
GUYON, FELICITE - MILLEGES, Richard
GWINN, Phebe Ann - FIELD, David

HACKNEY, Ariadne - MILLER, P. J.
HACKNEY, Esther - BENOIST, L. A.
HADWIN, Mary - HEELY, Thos.
HAHN, Sarah - BOYLE, Hugh
HAILMAN, Mary Ann - ABLE, S.
HALDEMAN, Margaret - HORINE, M. W.
HALE, E. - BELL, T. E.
HALFORD, Lucinda - YOUNG, Robert
HALL, Ann - BATTERTON, A. R.
HALL, Elizabeth A. - FRY, Thomas
HALL, Lucinda - SMILEY, Alfred
HALL, Timothia Ann - WARREN, Robt. E.
HALLEY, Sarah E. - BADGER, Albert
HAMILTON, Caroline Frances - DENNY,
   St. Clair
HAMILTON, E. - BRENHOLTZ, J.
HAMILTON, Eliza M. - VANVECHTEN,
   Abraham
HAMILTON, Jane - PARKER, Henry S.
HAMILTON, Mary - McKENZIE, Wallace
HAMMOND, Mary Jane - SHELTON,
   Charles D.
HANNA, Mary J. - HERN, Solomon S.
HAPPT, Anna Mary - EMGE, Peter
HARBORD, Eliza C. - NASH, Gilbert
HARDING, Nancy - CLAFLIN, William
HARDY, Sarah Ann - MARSH, Darius
HARKINS, Mrs. Mary - PRAGOFF, William
HARNER, Amelia Harriet - WHERRY,
   Joseph A.
HARPER, Ann E. - GRACE, Pierce
HARRALDSON, Eliza Frances - HURT, P.Y.
HARRIS, Amelia - PORTER, James H.
HARRIS, Maria Louisa - EWING, R.C.
HARRIS, Martha - PRICKETT, Abraham
HARRIS, Minerva - TODD, Ira
HARSELL, Harriet - FOGLE, Elisha
HARSHAW, Margaret A. - HICKS, B.B.
HARSHAW, Matilda - HATCH, Samuel

96

HART, Ann - STUART, Charles W.
HARTSHORN, Harriet - PHILLIPS, Nath'l
HARVEY, Priscilla - FINLEY, Asa
HARWOOD, Mariah - BACON, Edmund G.
HASTEN, Ann Eliza - WOODS, John C.
HAVERSTICK, Emilie - GEIGER, Wm. R.
HAWKINS, Julia A. - SEARS, Arthur E.
HAY, Aurora - CHOTEAU, Paul
HAY, Elizabeth - RALPH, George W.
HAY, Eulalie - GOFORTH, Wm. G.
HAY, Virginia - TILTON, Wm. P.
HAYDEN, Evaline - MADISON, James
HAYDON, Sarah - HAYDON, _____
HAYES, Griselda - MORELAND, Daniel
HAYNES (HYNES), Mary Jane -
   McCREERY, Phocion R.
HAYS, Joanah - BROWN, Azariah
HAZELTON, Eliza -RENFREW, John
HEADENBOURG, Emily Jane - BROWN,
   Morgan W.
HEALD, Mary S. - McCAUSLAND, David
HEALDT, Fredericka - REED, John H.
HELM, Matilda T. - FORD, Thomas D.
HELLER, Harriet Caroline - EDWARDS,
   Dorsson
HEMPSTEAD, Mrs. Clarisa C. - DETHIER,
   Louis
HEMPSTEAD, Cornelia - WILSON, John B.
HEMPSTEAD, Mary L. - LORIMIER, P.A.
HEMPSTEAD, Susan - GRATIOT, Henry
HENRIE, Angelique - TAYLOR, Daniel
HENRY, Christina - FOSTER, Robert
HENRY, Mary - SLAUGHTER, Thomas J.
HERRICK, Henrietta K. - VEITCH,
   Isaac McKendree
HERSHEY, Barbara Ann - JOHNSON, Samuel
HERTZOG, Ann - WICKLIFEE, Wm. N.
HERTZOG, Mary - DOUGHERTY, John
HERTZOG, Rachel W. - COOKE, Philip
   St. George
HESSER, Anastasia - HARDIN, Thomas
HIATT, Kate - HEARNE, Franklin P.
HICKMAN, Caroline - WINDSOR, H. H.
HICKMAN, Clarissa - FLOURNOY, Hoy
HIGGINS, Elenor - GILHULY, Bernard
HIGGINS, Winifred - PATTERSON, N.
HIGHLAND, Alesy Ann - LEMMON, George
HILER, Lydia - BAKER, George
HILL, Ann - VINCENT, Henry
HILL, Susan L. - RIDGELY, Stephen
HILLS, Julia Ann - FORBES, Leonard
HILLS, Harriet Rosetta - McILVAINE,
   Joseph

HISENOGGLE, Hannah - DEWEY, Walter
HIX, Eliza - KEYTE, James
HIX, Julia A. - SHEPHERD, George
   Washington
HIX, Laura A. - SAUNDERS, Daniel G.
HOBBS, Laura W. - HOPKINS, William
HOCKADAY, Amelia - STEPHENS, James L.
HODGE, Helen - WILLIAMSON, James
HODGKINSON, Margaret - HODGKINSON,
   John
HODGMAN, Marie - WOOD, William A.
HOFFA, Mrs. Catherine - FORSYTH,
   William M.
HOFFMAN, Amelia F. - ALEXANDER,
   E. B.
HOLDING, Mary Elizabeth - MATTHEWS,
   John S.
HOLLACHER, Appolonia - BINDER, John
HOLLAND, Sarah E. - HOYER, Edward
HOLLYMAN, Mary Ann - RUTTER, James
HOLMAN, Mrs. Eliza Ann - PATTON,
   Nathaniel
HOLMES, Caroline - ELY, Ezra Stiles
HOLMES, Elixa - RENWICK, William
HOLTZMAN, Eliza - HUTCHINGS, John
HOOD, Mary - BRADEN, John
HOOD, Mary - SLOANE, J. M.
HOOK, Nancy - WORKMAN, David
HOPKINS, Sarah A. D.- CONNELL,
   Wm. Fletcher
HOSTER, Caroline - JACOBY, Fred'k.
HOUSTON, Sarah Ann - SEDGWICK, Selser
HOUX, Elizabeth - McFARLAND, John
HOWARD, Elizabeth Flora - WASHBURN,
   Lewis
HOWARD, Mary - KANE, John
HOWELL, Nancy - BROWN, John
HOWIS, Mary - COPELAND, John
HOWDESHELL, Miss ___ - JONES, J.
HOY, Sarah D. - ORTON, Oliver
HOYT, Mary Ann - SCOTT, John W.
HUBBARD, Ann - SHACKELFORD, Richard
HUBERT, Celestia - KNIGHT, John A.
HUGGINS, Julia A. - DYER, Wm. F.
HUMPHRIES, Jane - KEY, George T.
HUNT, Eliza M. - SOULARD, James G.
HUNTER, Lucy - STICKNEY, Benjamin
HUNTINGTON, Eliza Irena - SALISBURY,
   Philander
HUNTINGTON, Martha - SMITH, Benj.
HUNT, Theodocia L. - STROTHER,
   George F.

HUTCHINGS, Eliza - TAYLOR, Dubart M.
HYDE, Sarah C. - LACY, Benjamin

INGRAHAM, Catherine G. - STAVELY,
   John W.
ISOM, Marcelite - DE GUIRE, Benjamin
ISRAEL, Miss ___ - RILEY, B.
IVINS, Mary S. - ANDERSON, Tom F.

JACKSON, Adelaide Frances - FIELDS,
   Henry
JACKSON, Julia Ann - BURCKHARTT,
   Matthias N.
JACKSON, Martha Ann - DOWNS, Wm. L. L.
JACKSON, Nancy - FRISTOE, Thomas
JACKSON, Permelia - RODGERS, Rev.
   Ebenezer
JACOB, Julia Ann - VANDIVER, John W.
JACOBS, Jane A. - LA COSSIT (DE LA
   COSSITT), H.
JAMES, Angeline - SMITH, James R.
JAMES, Mildred - EVANS, Augustus H.
JAMES, Rebecca - BROWN, Clement
JANUARY, Mary - COCHRAN, Marshall Stark
JARVAIS, Josephin - DYON, P. H. Leblanc
JAYNES, Matilda - WINN, John
JENNINGS, Eugenia Malvina - KERR,
   Augustus
JENNINGS, Sarah Maria - McKAY,
   Harrison B.
JOHNSON, Amanda - CASTLEMAN, W. S.
JOHNSON, Eliza - GILDERSLEEVE, Noah
JOHNSON, Eliza - LYONS, ___
JOHNSON, Elizabeth - WELLS, Peter
JOHNSON, Frances A. - AYRES, L. P.
JOHNSON, Margaret - DOWDALL, Robert W.
JOHNSON, Mary - MURDOCK, Francis B.
JOHNSON, Matilda - LEVI, Solomon J.
JOHNSTONE, Louisa A. - SELKIRK, Alexander
JONES, Agnes C. - HANENKAMP, R. P.
JONES, Cynthia Ann - SISSON, Edward
JONES, Eugenia B. - CUTHBERT, Samuel
JONES, Nancy Ann - SHORT, Evin
JONES, Mrs. Ursula - SNYDER, Jacob
JOURDAN, Catharine - BLAIR, James
JUDIE, Leonora A. - McPAUL, Charles

KAESER, Verena - VOLKER, Michael
KAVANAGH, Mrs. ___ CANOLE, Charles
KAYLOR (TAYLOR?), S. C. - WOOD, David

KEATEN, Mary - DeHODIAMONT, _____
KEATING, Martha - TAYLOR, W. W.
KEISTER, Mrs. Elizabeth - HAYWOOD,
   William H.
KEITH, Ellen M. - WHITE, William H.
KELLY, Ann C. - SMALL, Joel
KENNET, Nancy K. - SWON, John C.
KENNETT, Caroline - BEEBE, E. H.
KETCHUM, Eliza E. - BRICE, B. W.
KEYS, Mary - FULLER, Thomas
KIBBE, Harriet - BOST, John C.
KING, Ann - CHILDS, Caleb
KING, Serena A. - MUNSON, Rev. A.
KINGSBURY, Levinia - BOGGS, Thomas C.
KINKAID, E. - NEILL, Joseph
KIRBY, Sarah R. - COWLES, Wm. P.
KIZER, Elizabeth S. - CONNELLY,
   William W.
KLEIN, Phoebe Ann Eliza - RENSHAW,
   William
KNIGHT, Lucy - SNOW, Henry H.
KNOX, Nancy - HARDEMAN, John
KNOX, Sarah - MARSHALL, L. P.
KYLE, Ellen - STEPHENSON, James W.
KYLE, Harriet - PRICE, Christopher M.
KYRIE, Jane - HOOD, Richard

LABADIE, Mrs. Maria Antoinette -
   LITTLE, John
LaBARGE, Eliza - KICK, Charles
LaBARGE, Margaret - TAYLOR, Levi
LABEAU, Mme. ___ - L'ANDREVILLE, Andre
LA CHARITY, Mary - COLWELL, S. S.
LACKLAND, Lavinia M. - HEMPSTEAD,
   Stephen
LACROIX, Adeline - CHANDLER, Samuel B.
LaCROIX, Mrs. Julia - BOSTWICK, Oliver
LACY, Lydia - MOORE, G. W.
LAFLIN, Mary Ann - LIXON, Elias
LALAMIERE, Susan M. - WIER, Geo. F.
LAMB, Matilda - RICHARDS, R.K.
LAMBERT, Virginia - BORDOUX, Peter
LASHMUTT, Catherine - FONTAINE, A.M.
LAUCHLIN, Mary Jane - DARNES, Wm. P.
LAVERTY, Sarah Ann - GREEN, James
LAWRENCE, Eliza H. - GAY, David
LAWS, Mrs. Sarah - HILL, Ames
LEAR, Lavina - WILLSON, Robert
LEARNED, Susan H. - BRADY, Horace D.
LEBRUN, Louise - TELEE, L.M.F.
LEE, B. - THOMPSON, John W.
LEE, Jane - FINNEY, William

LEE, Jemima - SMITH, Oliver C.
LEE, Lydia - RECTOR, Stephen
LEE, Martha - PHILLIPS, Edward J.
LEE, Mary Eliza - FLEMING, Robert F.
LEE, Sophia - O'FALLON, Benj.
LeFAIVRE, Pelagie - RENSER, Isaac
LEFAVRE, Phillippine M. - FASSEU,
   Louis Ignace Antoine
LELAND, Lucinda - FLEMING, Robert K.
LELAND, Maria A. - RITCHIE, W. G.
LEPARD, Elizabeth - OLIVER, Obediah
LEROY, Helen - LANE, Nathaniel T.
LESLIE, Elizabeth B. - HAYDEN,
   Julius A.
LEVY, Jane - NEWMARK, A.
LEVY, Matilda - PEIXOTTO, D. C.
LEWIS, Agnes W. - CLARK, John C.
LEWIS, Elizabeth - FREELAND, Robert
LEWIS, Elzina - HUTCHINSON, John D.
LEWIS, Mary - HUGHES, L. F.
LEWIS, Mary Ann - HALLAM, Alexander
LEWIS, Mary Catherine - COLEMAN,
   Samuel
LEWIS, Mary H. C. - ASAY, Alexander B.
LEWIS, Sophronia - Stark, William
LIGHTFOOT, Mrs. Susan - DOYLE, Michael
LOCKE, Mary - PACKARD, Bryant A.
LOCKWOOD, Georgianna E. - WALKER,
   Orange
LOE, Catherine - HUFFAKER, George F.
LOISEL, Josephine - PAPIN, Hypolite
LOKER, Anna - LOKER, Wm. M.
LONDON, Mary Ann - JOPLING, John
LONG., Amelie - PENRICE, John S.
LONG, Mary E. - CLARDY, E. S.
LONGACRE, Isabella - LONGACRE, John
LOOMIS, Elizabeth C. - BETTS, Wm. B.
LOOMIS, Julia M. - MOREHOUSE, Legrand
LOPER, Sarah - CROSLER, Henry
LOTT, Emelina Louisa - SOUTHACK, Francis
LOVELL, Mary - RADFORD, Wm.
LOVING, Malinda - VANDEVER, G. P.
LUCKIE, Irene - BELL, John T.
LUYSTER, Mary Ann - WENDOVER, Joseph R.
LYNCH, Rosina - LINDSAY, Hiram
LYNN, Martha P. - ARMSTRONG, Clinton

McALISTER, Elizabeth (Mrs.) - CORBIN,
   Abel R.
McALISTER, Eliza Jane - CAIN, Jacob M.

McBETH, Angeline - SCOTT, Samuel S.
McBETH, Catherine A. - McNUTT, Samuel
McCARTAN, Mary - FERGUSON, Wm.
McCARTEN, Eleanor - KNAPP, George
McCARTAN, Sarah A. - TROWBRIDGE, Geo.
McCLAREY, Mary Magdalena - McNAIR, A.R.
McCLURE, Jane - WARNOCK, Mr. ____
McCOLLOCH, Nancy M. - THORNBURGH,
    Josiah
McCOMLEY, Phebe Ann - HIDDERN, Noah H.
McCONAPY, Eliza - DRIPS, Charles A.
McCORMICK, C. C. - MOORE, George W.
McCREERY, Acrata A. - HARGADINE,
    William A.
McCULLOH, Ann -BUTTS, John
McCULLOUGH, Margaret - FRYER, James H.
MACDONALD, Jennie - DEAN, Thomas A.
McDONALD, Phebe - HUNT, Robert
McDOUGAIL, Louisa A. - SMITH, John
McDOWELL, Eliza - BENTON, Thos. H.
McDOWELL, N. H. - BARTLETT, George W.
McELROY, Margaret - PETTIBONE, Henry
McFARLAND, Margaret - GIBBS, Jonathon H.
McGHEE, Caroline - POCOCKE, Wm. M.
McGHEE, Mary - SHARP, Benjamin F.
McKAY, Ellen - LEA, Isaac
McKEE, Mrs. Bridget Martha Roy -
    McKENZIE, Roderick Charles
McKEE, Mary - HOMES, Frederick
M'KENNEY, Mary Ann - CASSILY, P.
McLANAHAN, Nancy J. - WRIGHT, F. B.
McLANE, Hannah - GALLAGHER, Bernard
McLANE, E. H. - HOOD, G. W.
McLANE, Juliet - GARESCHE, P. Baudoy
McLEAN, Miss ____ - SEHON, Edward
McLENAHAN, Lucy Ann - ISAACS, Robert
McLEON, Ellen Elizabeth - TAYLOR,
    Jeremiah R.
McREA, Mary - MAGENIS, A. L.
McVICKER, Frances Brenton - McDONOUGH,
    Augustus Rodney

MACKLIF, Julia F. - WILCOX, Seymour B.
MACKLOT, Marie Isabelle - WALLACE,
    Hamilton W.
MACRAE, Eugene Louisa - AUSTIN,
    Charles H.
MADDOX, J. B. - McBRIDE, A. S.
MAHEW, Eleanor - FINENTELLE, Charles
MAITLAND, Margaret J. - ANDERSON, Geo. C.

MALLERSON, ____ - MITTELBERGER, John C.
MALLEY, Julia - RONEY, Michael
MALOTT, Edna Maria - DETCHEMENDY,
    Julius A.
MARCIA, Francis E. - BUTTERFIELD,
    Francis A.
MARKER, Frances Jane - KRITZER, Mr.__
MARKS, Elizabeth - COE, Alven
MARKS, Sarah M. - RUSH, James
MARION, Sarah E. - RHODES, Jacob
MARS, Almira Jane - WILLIAMS, Saml. R.
MARSH, Nancy - HEATH, Jesse W.
MARSHALL, Nancy -McCURDY, Fleming B.
MARTIN, Frances Ann - WRIGHT, Henry C.
MARTIN, Julia - JOHNS, James
MARTIN, Nancy - CALDWELL, Larkin G.
MASON, Mary Murray - DASHIELL,
    Alfred H.
MASSEI, Judith Ann - MILAM, James V.
MATHEWS, Mary M. - STOCKER, Wm. H.
MATTHEWS, Levina - GLENN, Tyre W.
MATTHEWS, Mary Jane - SABIN, Elijah
MAXEY, Rebecca Jane Elizabeth Martha
    Ann - VANLANDINGHAM, William
MAYNARD, Cornelia J. - BEER, Henry J.
MAXWELL, Adeline - STETTINIUS, Joseph
MAY, Martha Ann - KURLBAUM, Julius W.J.
MEANS, Eliza C. - SEELY, C. C.
MEDLEY, Eliza - MALONE, Richard
MEDLEY, Sarah - DALY, James
MEECH, Eliza W. - BIRGE, Henry W.
MEIER, Susanna - BOWLES, Samuel
MELLON, Jane E. - McMULLEN, Oliver H.
MENARD, Theresse B. - CHOUTEAU,
    Francis
MENARD, Virginia - ST. VRAIN, S.
MERINOT, Angelica - PESCAY, Julius
METCALF, Sarah - CALLAHAN, Henry C.
MILLER, Elenor A. - GUY, John R.
MILLER, Elizabeth Latimer -BILL, Charles
MILLER, Julia - CLARK, William G.
MILLER, Margaretta - FIELD, R. R.
MILLER, Sally C. - WINSTON, Thomas
MILLER, Sarah - McCORD, John
MILLER, Sarah C. - SCOTT, John R.
MILLER, Sydney - CLOUSE, George
MILLS, Mrs. Mary G. - FLOOD, John J.
MITCHELL, Annett - HOLLIDAY, John D.
MITCHELL, Caroline - HALL, John
MITCHELL, Elizabeth - BLAIR, John A.G.
MOORE, Elizabeth - WATERS, Samuel

MOORE, Martha Isabella - CRAIG, Josiah C.
MOORE, Mary E. - BURKE, John
MORIN, Natalie - MANTIAL, Castara
MORISON, Olivia - VON SCHRADER, Frederick
MORRIS, Anna - GREGORY, Richard A.
MORRIS, Caroline C. - AUSTIN, Wm. J.
MORRIS, L. - GENSLER, Samuel
MORRISON, Catherine - LAY, James H.
MORRISON, Elouisa - PHILIPS, Joseph
MORRISON, Eloise P. - KAYSER, Alexander
MORRISON, Emily - HAY, Andrew
MORTON, Ann - STOCKTON, Richard G.
MORTON, Ellen - TRACY, Alfred
MORTON, Sophia - TRACY, Chas. F.
MORTON, _____, DEVRICKS, John
MOSBY, Mary Jane - SAVAGE, Rev. F.A.
MOSS, Sarah - TUTTLE, Gilpin
MULDROW, Ellen - CURTIS, Charles H.
MULFORD, Elizabeth - PILKINGTON, Samuel B.
MULINS, Jane - ADKINSON, Samuel
MULLANPHY, Ann - BIDDLE, Thos.
MULLEN, Margaret - BARRY, James
MULLINS, Judith E. - TRABUE, Joseph
MUN, Rachel - KETCHUM, Samuel (David)
MUNRO, Eleanor - HALL, John
MUNRO, Ellen - TOOLEY, Porter
MUNRO, Sarah - BENSON, Ira
MURDOCK, Elizabeth - REESE, David R.
MURPHY, Elvira - JOHNSON, John
MURPHY, Jane T. - WALKER, Geo. A.
MURRAY, Isabella J. - HENDRIX, Adam
MURRAY, Mrs. Priscilla - RICHARDSON, Freeman
MURRY, Nancy A. - McGARY, James D.
MYERS, Matilda A. - ADAMS, Wm. H.

NASH, Mary Virginia Stith - LOCKWOOD, Samuel Drake
NEAL, Mrs. ___ - GOODMAN, Montgomery
NESTER, Nancy - STOKES, William
NEWMAN, Margaret C. - YOUNT, Geo.
NICHOL, Catherine - McKINSEY, James
NICHOLLS, Margaret - DOUGHTY, James W.
NEWTON, Martha Ann - PUTNEY, Amos C.
NIMAN, Ellen - LINDELL, Peter, Jr.
NORRIS, Mrs. Maria - DAVIS, Rolla
NOYES (NOYCE), Sarah C. - MONTGOMERY, Thos. J.

O-ARK, Eliza - HIBLER, Ephraim
O'FALLON, Mrs. Sophia - McBRIDE, F.C.
OGLESBY, Malvina - HOUX, William
O'HARA, Margaret - METCALFE, William
O'HARA, Margaret A. - WHITLOCK, Andrew S.
OLDRUM, Elizabeth - LUNDY, P. F.
O'NEIL, Matilda - BRANT, Henry B.
ORME, Martha - RAWLINGS, Hiram
ORR, Mrs. M. - CAULK, Isaac
OSGOOD, Marcella - WATERS, Absolem
OSBORNE, Jemima - MING, James M.
OTEY, Nannie L. - McCLELLAND, James Bruce
OWEN, Mary - HANNA, Robert
OWENS, Jane - MAXFIELD, E. C.
OWINGS, Sarah - COHEN, Albert B.

PADDOCK, Julia - REILY, Henry
PAGE, Susan - MANNING, B. F.
PALMER, Eliza C. - GARDNER, A. M.
PARCELL, Milvina - FUSS, Peter
PARIS, Adeline - GOLL, Cephas
PARKER, America - EDMONDSON, Julius
PARKER, Mary E. - SPENCER, Charles L.
PARKER, Sarah - HUME, Michael
PARKS, Emeline - HUNTER, Charles G.
PARKS, Rebecca - WINN, James
PARMER, Ann - MOORE, Daniel Sharp Delany
PARRISH, Elizabeth J. - McGIRK, Andrew
PARROT, Matilda M. - TURNER, Jos. P.
PARVIN, Elizabeth - MULFORD, Charles
PASTUER, Virginia Ann - VANSANT, Isaia
PASQUIER, Virginia Pelagie - McDONALD, John W.
PATTERSON, Miss ___ - PURDIN, William
PATTON, Elizabeth - McCLURE, Samuel
PATTON, Frances Noyle - KENNEDY, R.V.
PAUL, Mary Ann - McKEE, Isaac H.
PEALER, Martha Ann - KNAUSE, Henry
PEEBELS, Mary Ann - KIRTLEY, Sinclair
PEEBLES, Eliza - RYLAND, Edwin M.
PENNEMAN, Mrs. Eliza - STARK, Horatio
PERDREAUVILLE, Marie Antoinette Adele GRATIOT, J. P. B.
PETERSON, Margaret - NELSON, Thomas
PETTIBONE, Mariah - HUNT, Ezra
PEYTON, Harriet Jane - WADE, John M.
PHILIP, Margaret - FILEKIL, John
PHILIPSON, Esther - CLARY, R. E.
PHILLIPS, Susan - SLADE, Wm. M.
PHILLIPSON, Amanda - CLARKE, Wm. H.

PICKRELL, Caroline Saloma - RISQUE, Ferd. W.
PIERCE, Lucy M. - MILLS, R. B.
PIPKIN, Frances E. - LONG, John F.
PITTS, Mary Ann - LEAMAN, G. A.
PLANT, Nancy - CASEY, James
PLATT, Angelina - REED, Henry S.
POGUE, Mary Jane - DIX, Edw. H.
POLK, Eveline M. - CULTON, D. M.
POND, Hannah - BIGHAM, David
POOL, Elizabeth - WALTON, John
POOL, Mary - LEAR, Zachariah
POOLE, Ann - CARLILE, Stephen
POORMAN, Louisa - GREGG, Leonard
POPE, Penelope - ALLEN, Beverly
PORTER, Frances A. - BEEBE, Edward H.
PORTER, Lydia Gould - HARLOW, Saml. S.
PORTER, Mary Ellen - OWENS, Stephen B.
POST, Eliza - BRECKENRIDGE, John
POSTALL, Mary A. - HIVER, Abraham
POSTEN, Emiline - HILL, John W.
POTEET, Mrs. C. - BATES, David G.
POTTER, Adeline E. - PECK, Chas. A.
POTTER, Sarah E. - HART, George
POWELL, Ann M. - STUART, W.H.H.
POWERS, Rachel - JACOBSON, F.M.
PRATTE, Emilia - CROOKS, Ramsay
PRATTE, Pelagie - BOGY, Louis V.
PRATTE, Theresa - ALEXANDER, Walter B.
PREMBLAY, Adelline - TURCOTTE, Narcisse
PRENTIS, Mrs. Caroline Cornelia - MAYO, Peyton Randolph
PRESTON, Caroline L. - WOOLLEY, A. F.
PRESTON, Josephine - ROGERS, J.
PREWITT, Mary Jane - SWITZER, Wm. N.
PRICE, Ann - PRICE, John
PRICE, Martha A. - WELLS, Jno. W.
PRICE, Martha M. - MASON, Luther
PRIMM, Mary A. - DUHRING, Andrew
PRINCE, Sarah - JONES, R. P.
PROCTOR, America - ALDRIDGE, Alexi
PULLIAM, Ann - CHEEK, William
PULLIAM, Ann R. - WILSON, John
PULLIAM, Martha M. - NOWLIN, Peyton Jr.

RADFORD, Mary - KEARNEY, S. N.
RAY, Mary Ann - CLARKSTON, Caleb
READ, Clarissa - HOVEY, Edwin
READ, Elizabeth - LAMB, Joseph
RECTOR, Mrs. Eliza S. - DADE, John

REED, Maria - NEGUS, Isaac Jr.
REEVES, Jeannette - LEONARD, Abiel
REILLY, Ann M. - MAXWELL, James G.
RENNICK, Ann - MANN, Alfred
RENNOLDS, Nancy - BURNBANKS, Elijah
REYNOLDS, Ann - HANNA, James
REYNOLDS, Julia - JONES, Thomas
REYNOLDS, Margaret A. - BELT, Henry B.
RICHARD, Mrs. Mary V. - MILBURN, Wm.
RICHARDS, Elizabeth V. - JOHNSTON, Edward
RICHARDS, Sydney - OSBURN, Nicholas C.
RICHARDSON, Betsy - ELLINGTON, Wm.
RICHARDSON, Martha - JEWETT, Jackson
RICHESON, Julia E. - DINKLE, James M.
RICHMOND, Laura E. - HAVEN, Chas. H.
RICKETTS, M. Louisa - STEINFELD, John
RICKMAN, Mary - MURRELL, Jos. P.
RIDDICK, Francis E. - BILLON, Charles P.
RIDDICK, Virginia C. - BROOKS, Edward
RIDDLE, Catharine B. - STONE, Wm.
RIDDLE, Eliza - FIELD, J. M.
RIDGELY, Octavia - SHAW, Lyman B.
RIFFLE, Italia - ATHEY, P.
RIFFLE, Mary - LANGTON, Jeremiah
RIGGS, Julia - DRAPER, Daniel
RILEY, Margaret - BOLIO, Louis
RION, Margaret A. - REED, Joseph D.
RIPPEY, Mary - TURNER, J. B.
RISQUE, Harriet J. - HUTTER, G. C.
RITTER, Eliza R. A. - BROWN, Benj. B.
ROBARDS, Martha Ann - CARSON, Henry S.
ROBBINS, Emily - GREELY, C. S.
ROBBINS, Savinia - MOORE, Jonas
ROBERS, Mrs. Rebecca - HAMMOND, John
ROBERT, Eleanor - RIDGELY, Franklin L.
ROBERT, Josephine S. - HUNT, Philemon
ROBERT, Miss ___ - COURTOIS, Louis
ROBERTS, Miss ___ - BATTE, Mr. ___
ROBERTSON, Mrs. Eliza - CARLISLE, John
ROBINS, Mary W. - POWELL, William
ROBINSON, Catherine Elizabeth - TRAEGER, Charles August
ROBINSON, Mrs. Eliza - YATES, John D.
ROBINSON, Joanna - HUDSPETH, Abijah
ROBINSON, Mary - CRAWFORD, Thomas L.
RODGERS, Emily - HUDSON, Wayne C.
ROGERS, Lydia R. - SHREVE, H. M.
ROGERS, Susannah - HALDERMAN, John
ROMANS, Catherine B. - EVANS, John P.
ROMINE, Amanda - EMMERSON, Alexander R.

RONEY, Sarah Jane - KOHN, Marcus
ROOKER, Lutetia - ROOKER, C. F.
ROSS, Mary Ann L. - JAMES, Wm.
ROUTSANG, Elizabeth - KENDAL, ___
ROWND, Ann Morris - TURPIN, Wm. R.
RUBEY, Elizabeth A. - PATTON, John W.H.
RULAND, Eliza - KERR, James D., Jr.
RULAND, Susan C. - BAILY, David
RUNKLE, Frances V. - BEAN, James M.
RUNTER, Ella E. - LAMPTON, James A.H.
RUSSELL, Eliza - KEW, William
RUSSELL, Margaret C. - GARRETT, Fredk.
RUSSELL, Mary - INNES, Charles
RUSSELL, Mrs. R. - PARKER, Edward
RUTTER, Emily - RUTLAND, James

SAMUEL, Clara - SILVERBURG, Robert
SANDERS, Arabella - FISHER, Edward
SANDFORD, Catawea - WORLEY, Chas.
   Woodruff
SANDFORD, Sciota - GATLIN, N.C.
SANDSBURY, Mary - KELSO, Harrison R.
SANFORD, Henrietta C. - CLARK, John B.
SANFORD, Nancy - McQUEEN, J. P. Dudley
SANFORD, Orphana - LAWRENCE, Elias D.
SANFORD, Virginia E. - RANSOM, S.H.
SANGUINET, Adele - THOLOZAN, J. Eli
SANGUINET, Carolina - COZENS, Horatio
SAPPINGTON, Margaret B. - DEAN, Henry C.
SAUGRAIN, Eliza - KENNERLY, James
SAUNDERS, Louisa T. - FOSTER, Robert C.
SAVAGE, Mary G. - CADY, Cyril C.
SAWYER, Rosanna - LEAK, Wm. S.
SAVER, Louisa - SCHOEFFLER, Charles C.
SCHULTIZE, Christine - GRENAR, Louis
SCOFIELD, Emeline - PAPIN, Silvestre
SCOLEY, Eveline B. - MANNING, John F.
SCOTT, Ann Maria Caroline - SHACKELFORD,
   Richard C.
SCOTT, Fanny - McKNIGHT, Thomas
SCOTT, Mary - MUNN, Ira Y.
SCOTT, Mary - HARBISON, John
SCUDDER, Mary E. - WEIRICK, R. C.
SEARCEY, Altazena - HILL, Harvey
SEAWELL, Nannie P. - HAMILTON, Rev.
   Alexander L.
SEELEY, Hannah - HILL, D. B.
SELDEN, Pink - McPHEETERS, Wm.
SEVAYES, Mrs. Carmel - NALLEY, Alexander
SHACKELFORD, Anna Peyre - DINNIES, John C.
SHAFFNER, Elenora - COGSWELL, Oscar B.
SHANNON, Adeline B. - COOK, Robert
SHANNON, Emily C. - CHENAULT, Wm. M.
SHANNON, Sara Lavenia - SAMUEL, Wm. P.

SHAW, Isidora - LaBEAUME, C. Edmund
SHAW, Mary - McLARD, James
SHAW, Nancy - SAMUEL, Presley
SHEAFE, Auguste Haven - OSBORN, Wm. H.
SHEPERD, Lydia - GLASSCOCK, John
SHEPHERD, Rebecca Isadora - MONROE,
   John T.
SHEPPARD, Nicy - BENNETT, Wm. M.
SHERMAN, Lucinda - MAXWELL, Thomas
SHEVINIL, Jane - HOOKER, William
SHORE, Sarah W. - BROWN, Andrew J.
SHREVE, Harriet S. - REEL, J. W.
SHUMATE, Elizabeth A. - BARTHOLOMEW,
   Collins W.
SIMMONS, Cammelio - McMANUS, William
SIMONDS, Mary - WATSON, Ebenezer
SIMONDS, Miss ___ - FRAZER, John
SIMPSON, Eliza - BARRETT, J. R.
SINGLETON, Anna - SMITH, Wm.
SIZER, Mary - WOODWARD, Edward K.
SKELTON, Martha A. E. - BENSON, James
   R.
SKILLMAN, Mary Jane - ELLET, John G.
SKINNER, Hannah M. - FULTON, James
SKINNER, Nannie W. - BARBER, Wm. B.
SKINNER, Sophie - LEE, John
SLACK, Elizabeth - FORREST, William
SLADE, Mrs. Eloise - McLURKEN, Thos.
SLATER, Caroline - LOWE, John
SLATER, Elizabeth - ANDREWS, John
SLAVENS, Elizabeth - McCLURE, Wm.
SMARR, Susan F. - COFER, Thomas A.
SMITH, Adaline - THOMAS, Jesse B.
SMITH, Ann - MATHEWS, Rev. John
SMITH, Ann - CARSON, John B.
SMITH, Aurelia Clarissa - GRAINGER,
   William
SMITH, Caroline - FIELDS, Jesse
SMITH, Dorothea - BAKER, John E.
SMITH, Eliza - HEMPSTEAD, Lewis E.
SMITH, Elizabeth - BELT, James Walter
   P.
SMITH, Jane C. S. - ROBIDOUX, Felix
SMITH, Julia - MALONE, Calvin
SMITH, Martha Frances - HARRIS, E. D.
SMITH, Mrs. Mary - BISHOP, A. K.
SMITH, Mary Ann - WARBURTON, John
SMITH, Mrs. Rebecca - GREEN, William
SMITH, Sophronia - CARUTHERS, Samuel
SMITHERS, Mary - KILPATRICK, T. J.
SNELL, Narcissa - RORER, Samuel N.
SNODGRASS, Theresa - CHAYTOR, Joseph
SNOW, Lucinda - POGUE, Robert
SNYDER, Anna Maria - DORWART, David

SNYDER, Eliza - HERYER, Jacob
SOFFLIN, Mary - HOFFMAN, Frederick
SOUTH, Eliza- HOLTZCLAW, Richard
SOUTHGATE, Mary L. - HAWTHORN, Jacob
SOUTHWICK, Mary Jane - STEWART, Wm.
SPALDING, Julia - REYNOLDS, Wm. T.
SPARKS, Charlotte T. - JACKSON, John
SPARKS, Sarah - DAGGET, John D.
SPEAR, Julia M. - PLUMP, Erich
SPENCER, Nancy Ann - RODGERS, Jesse H.
SPORTSMAN, Mary Ann - USHER, Saml. W.
SPRANGLEY, Harriet - ZAFF, Godfred
SPROULE, Martha Jane - BAILEY, Thompson L.
SPROUT, Mrs. Mary - DeBRUEN, John
SPURR, Susan - LINK, John Henry
SQUIRE, Julia - WOOLDRIDGE, Tilden W.
STAATS, Anna W. - LAFFLIN, Sylvester Hall
STAMPS, Bettie - RICE, Anapias
STANLEY, Frances Ann - OSBORNE, John J.
STAPP, Malinda - BLACKWELL, Robert
STARK, Susan - GRIMSLEY, Thornton
STARKS, Leonice - TULL, Thomas W.
STARR, Clarissa B. - GEYER, Henry S.
STARR, Emily - GENTRY, Ceato C.
STEPHENSON, Elvira Amanda - STARR, William E.
STEPHENSON, Martha - BROWN, Joseph
STERETT, Mary E. - HIGGINS, W. W.
STEVENS, Eliza J. - CUMMINS, H. F.
STIBBS, Mrs. Ellen - BALL, Albert
STINER, Charlotte E. - SANDER, John
STIR, Ceolida - BASEY, Henry
STIVERS, America - HAYES, Westley P.
STODDARD, Adeline - PECK, Ruluph
STODDARD, Jane M. - PAGE, Francis W.
STODDARD, Sarah - TRACY, Alfred
STOWELL, Louisa - ALVORD, J. N.
STRACZER, Mrs. Mary - CONROY, James
STTARNS (sic), Rebecca L. - ARTHUR, John
SULLIVAN, Mary - WALKER, James B.
SUMMERVILLE, Nancy G. - FARMER, N.
SUTTON, Frances - POPE, Orris
SWAIN, Sarah E. - OTIS, Benj. F.
SWAN, Mrs. Susan - LEFFINGWELL, Hiram W.
SYLVIA, Amelia - RUSSELL, Richard

TABBS, Mary C. - GANTT, Thomas T.
TALBOT, Mary J. - DEWEES, Nimrod
TALBOT, Sophia - DAVIDSON, John C.
TARLTON, Jane - McGEE, Hugh

TAYLOR, Amelia - YOUNGER, Charles
TAYLOR, Ann Elizabeth Paxton - REILLY, J. P.
TAYLOR, Ellen - DESHLER, David
TAYLOR, Emily - TAYLOR, John S., Jr.
TAYLOR, Harriet - WELLS, John
TAYLOR, Louisa S. - ARNOLD, Thomas J.
TAYLOR, Maria Louisa - HERNDON, James H.
TAYLOR, Mary Jane - MONTAGUE, Joseph
TAYLOR (KAYLOR?), S. C. - WOOD, David
TEESE, Sarah A. - ADAMS, Rudolph
TESSON, Mrs. Eliza - BRIGHT, Josiah
THATCHER, Julia Ann - HAVEN, Charles H.
THOMAS, Caroline - JENNINGS, N. A.
THOMAS, Elizabeth A. - KING, George
THOMAS, Mary - SHEPARD, Elihu H.
THOME, Martha - SMITH, Dalzell
THOMPSON, Anna - WATSON, Samuel R.
THOMPSON, Christine Nancy - OWENS, Elias
THOMPSON, Delia A. - STOUT, Benj. F.
THOMPSON, Eunice A. - HALLEY, Presley W.
THOMPSON, Margaret - REED, John D.
THOMPSON, Mary P. - SOWERS, Peter J.
THOMPSON, Mrs. Sophia Porter - LEA, Rev. Thomas D.
THOMSON, Elizabeth - WOLFE, J. B.
THORBURN, Jessie - DALRYMPLE, Wallace W.
THRALL, Minerva - PULLIAM, Wm. M.
THRESHLY, Emily L. - AUD, Frances L.
TIMBERLAKE, Mrs. Margaret - EATON, John H.
TIMON, Eleanor - KENNEDY, John
TIMON, Rosa T. M. - DALY, Michael
TISON, Adele - McGILL, Theodore
TODD, Elizabeth - BURNHAM, Foster
TODD, Elizabeth - GIBSON, Isaac W.
TODD, Spicy - WILSON, Pliny
TOOLEY, Mary - WHITE, William
TOWER, Mary L. - LITTLETON, M.
TRAINER, Mary Ann (Ana) - WARDEN or WARREN, John
TRAVERSE, Susanna - LEWIS, Joshua
TREGASKIS, Elizabeth Anne - EMBREE, Jas. H.
TRIGG, Elizabeth - THORNTON, John
TRIGG, Susannah - CLARK, Bennett H.
TRIPLETT, Ann Todd - McFADIN, James M.
TRUESDALL, Nancy - McKEE, Hiram
TUFTS, Lucy - WELSH, George S.
TURNER, Catherine Ann - TERRILL, James H.
TURNER, Sally Ann - DOWTHIT, Green L.
TURNER, Mary - PIERCE, Peter
TUTHILL, Mary S. - COLLINS, Morris
TYNNELL, Mrs. Jane - RICHARDS, Lewis

UNDERHILL, Augusta Antoinette - MARCH, E. C.

VACHARD, Genevieve - BUSTIN, David
VAIL, Julia Frances - HASTINGS, S.W.
VALDES, Carmelita - LIGHTNER, Isaac
VALLE, Mary - LAGRAVE, Antoine
VANDENBURGH, Jane Ann - MOTT, John H.
VANDERBURGH, Frances Sydney - SOMES, Joseph
VAN ZANDT, Laura Carnes - GARESCHE, Alexander
VENABLES, Matilda - BROWN, Robert
VIRDEN, Anne S. - SULLIVAN, Geo. W.
VON PFISTER, Elizabeth R. - KID, Wm. I.

WADDLE, F. - TILLMAN, Charles
WADDLE, Mrs. Poupon - LEE, Elliott
WADSWORTH, Martha - GOODWIN, Geo. W.
WAINWRIGHT, Martha G. - WITHNELL, John
WAITE, Louisa - STANHOPE, John B., Jr.
WALKER, Mrs. Matilda - TAYLOR, Nathaniel P.
WALKER, Sarah - GREIG, Wm.
WALKER, Sarah Ann - COLE, John
WALLER, Mary Amelia - RANKIN, T. M.
WALLS, Emily - VANDEVENTER, P. L.
WALTER, Ann - HILL, David B.
WALTON, Evy D. - COOK, John
WALTON, S. - HANLEY, M. F.
WARD, Elizabeth - CREWS, Samuel
WARD, Georane E. - MERRITT, J.D.
WARD, Laura B. - TAYLOR, Thomas J.
WARDEN, Mary Frances - MUIRFELDT, H.W.
WARDER, Mary A. - RANNELLS, Charles
WARE, Mary Anne - VAN NORTWICK, Ira
WARE, Sarah E. - NEIL, Robert
WARRANCE, Catharine K. - BALES, John
WARRANCE, Priscilla H. - MURRAY, John G.
WARREN, Elizabeth A. - WILLINGS, George W.
WARREN, Margaret - COATS, Alfred A.
WASH, Frances - GOODE, George W.
WASHINGTON, Mary - MILLER, William
WATERFIELD, Martha A. - TAYLOR, Joseph M.
WATKINS, Sarah A. - THAYER, S. F.
WATSON, Eliza - FITZWILLIAM, Thomas
WATSON, Margaret - WATKINS, Nathan W.
WATSON, Melinda A. - FONTAINE, Thomas L.
WAYFIELD, Anne Eliza - BYLAND, Edward M.
WEBSTER, Catherine - PROVER, Robert J.
WEEKS, Harriet C. - MEADE, D. E.

WELCH, Amanda M. F. - SELLERS, Isaiah
WELDIN, Mary C. - BURBBYGE, J. B.
WELLS, Miss ___ - WHITE, George
WELLS, Emely Elenor - MILES, Edmund
WEST, Clarissa - WHERRY, Daniel Boone
WEST, Louise - HOWARD, Thomas A.
WEST, Victoria - RICHMOND, Volney
WESTCOTT, Kate A. - ALLEN, Henry
WETHERILL, Margaret H. - WOODWORTH, A.L
WETMORE, Roxanna - BACON, George T.
WHEELER, Mathilda C. - VANHORN, Nathan
WHITE, Catherine B. - GOSHEE, James W.
WHITE, Jane E. - ALLEN, John A.
WHITE, Mary L. - TWICHELL, S.
WHITE, Pauliny - BRADY, Peter
WHITEHEAD, Elizabeth - KINDLER, John
WHITNEY, Myra Clark - GAINES, E. P.
WIDEMAN, Paty Pincke - BEAL, James A.
WILCOX, Caroline - YOUNG, Nelson A.
WILCOX, Julia L. - YOUNG, John
WILD, Anna - WARD, Porter
WILLIAMS, Abigail - FARNESWORTH, Alden
WILLIAMS, Elizabeth M. - RUNDLETT, John
WILLIAMS, Harriet Peerce - KELLY, R.N.
WILLIAMS, Sarena - GREEN, Samuel
WILLSON, Martha A. - SMYZER, George
WILMANS, Mary Theodosia - BARRET, Wm. James
WILSON, Ann - WILT, Christian
WILSON, Catherine W. - LUKE, J. W.
WILSON, Ellen - POWELL, Joseph
WILSON, Ellen - BARNHART, John
WILSON, Jane - POWELL, Peter
WILSON, Jane - TODD, Albert
WILSON, Jane M.D. - COPELIN, John R.
WILSON, Louise J. - RAGAN, George
WILSON, Margaret - LAMONT, Daniel
WILSON, Martha Ann - SMITH, Lewis
WILSON, Rachel - ALBRIGHT, Jacob W.
WILSON, Sarah Elizabeth - BENOIST, Louis A.
WINCHELL, Sarah M. - DRYDEN, John D.S.
WINDSOR, Caroline - MANTZ, Charles A.
WINN, Rebecca - PATTERSON, David
WISE, Ann Eliza - POPE, R. B.
WISHART, Jane B. - DE CAMPS, Wm.
WITHERS, Maria - MASSEY, Benj. F.
WOLF, Anna Catherine - MOORE, Wm.
WOLFSKILL, Elizabeth - LUCAS, B.F..
WOOD, Lucinda - TOWNSEND, Benj. F.
WOOD, Martha - LEAR, John
WOOD, Rachel J. - McKINNEY, Samuel T.
WOODBURY, Mary E. - BLAIR, Montgomery
WOODSON, Paulina B. - MILLER, Wm. H.
WORKMAN, Agnes - VICARS, John

WORTHINGTON, Martha Augusta - ENGLISH, James Lawrence
WRIGHT, Anna Maria - SANDS, S. G.
WRIGHT, Letitia - GERARD, John B.
WRIGHT, Mary Jane - LOKER, C. R.
WRIGHT, Sarah Ann - LOCKWOOD, J. H.
WYMER, Elizabeth - GRINSTEAD, Nathan
WYMER, Mrs. Rebecca - WHALEY, William

YATES, Georgia Ellen - LOWRY, Wm. F.
YEATMAN, Anna Maria - ANDERSON, W.C., Jr.
YEATMAN, Elizabeth - MORGAN, Henry
YOSTI, Marie - POTTER, John C.
YOUNG, Ann F. - ARTHUR, John
YOUNG, Catherine - NICHOLS, Arthur
YOUNGER, Eleanor - ALLEN, S. B.

* * * * *

ADDENDA

These marriages have not been checked in the counties where the marriages were supposed to have taken place. Lack of time, inability to get records, etc. account for their not being checked, and they are included in hope they may represent a "missing" marriage for some reader.

COUNTY: Buchanan

TILDEN, John of St. Louis	MAYES, Maria L. n.d.	HORL 28 May 1846
BIRCH, James H., Jr.	BULLOCK, Bettie T. (late Thos.) of Woodford Co., KY at Plattsburg 6th inst., Rev. Sam'l P. Johnson	STGAZ 12 May 1852
DAWSON, John M.	GUYNAND, Elizabeth 30 March, Judge Wyatt	STGAZ 7 April 1852
DOYON, Francis X.	ROULEAU, Mary Matilda 9 May, Rev. Scanlon	STGAZ 12 May 1852
HARRINGTON, James of St. Louis County	O'DONAGHUE, Anne Jane of St. Joseph 31 March, Rev. Thos. Scanlon	STGAZ 7 April 1852
HURLEY, Maurice	CROWLEY, Mary ? , Rev. Scanlon	STGAZ 12 May 1852
JOHNSTON, James Y. of DeKalb Co.	LUCAS, Martha A. (Wm.) formerly Hardin Co., KY 18th, no minister	STGAZ 26 May 1852
LOCKWOOD, S.	FARRAR, Rosanne A. H. 5th inst., Rev. Holmes	STGAZ 11 Feb. 1852
MORRISON, Maurice	MAXEY, Johanna 25 April, Rev. Thos. Scanlon	STGAZ 12 May 1852
NAPIER, E. J.	McCLELLAND, Mary 17 June, Rev. Wm. Holmes	STGAZ 23 June 1852

PENICK, William R.	GRIGG, Amanda (Dr. Edw. of Kalamazoo, MI 11th inst., Rev. J. Hickman	STGAZ 14 Jan. 1852
WASHBURN, Joseph	OLIVER, Emma Jane 11th inst., Milton E. Lash?	STGAZ 17 Mar. 1852

Cape Girardeau County

HARRIS, Thomas M. of St. Francois	HENDERSON, Margaret (Cyrus) of Cape Girardeau 4th inst., Rev. Robt. G. Barrett	OSD-STLH 17 May 1843
LITTLE, Henry	JOHNSON, Mary 7th, Rev. A. Munson	HORL 28 May 1846
McPHERSON, Franklin	LITTLE, Nancy 7th, Rev. A. Munson	HORL 28 May 1846
McNEELY, George N.	BROWN, Martha A. 4th, Rev. A. Munson	HORL 18 Dec. 1845
WELCH, Elias	BAST, Serene J. 12th	HORL 26 March 1846
STEVENSON, Kennedy	CLODFELTER, Elizabeth 4th, Rev. A. Munson	HORL 18 Dec. 1845

Clay County

TURNER, Col. Winslow of Plattsburg	POLLARD, Emily (Thomas M.) formerly of Franklin Co., VT n.d., no minister	JINQ 9 Dec. 1841

Lincoln County

MURRAY, S. F. of Bowling Green	WELLS, Fanny (Carty) of Palmyra 20 Jan., Rev. David Diamond	PWH 3 Feb. 1848

Monroe County

ELGIN, Joseph F.	ABERNATHY, Joannah (James R.) of and at Paris, Monroe Co. 11th, Elder Henry Thomas	FULT 20 July 1849
QUARLES, Benj. L.	YOUNG, Sarah E. (Rev. John F.) all of and at Florida, Mo. 3rd, Rev. R. M. Spencer	FULT 4 May 1849
GLENN, Dr. Hugh J.	ABERNATHY, H. (James R.) all of Paris, Mo., 14th no minister (PWH gives her as Nancy, min. Elder Henry Thomas)	FULT 30 March 1849

106

Morgan County
MINOR, G.
attorney at law

McCLANAHAN, Henrietta J.
(Capt. J.), 21 Dec., Rev. Chism

JINQ
28 Dec. 1843

Pettis County
MERCER, John D.
of Tennessee

PEMBERTON, Judith B. (George)
of Pettis Co.
27th, Rev. David Hogan

WEMI
10 Jan. 1839

St. Francois County
BRADY, Jos. J.
all of Farmington

BOYCE, Mary C.
10 Dec., Rev. Amos Rogers

HORL
18 Dec. 1845

Schuyler County
CUSTER, James W.

MILLAN, Susanna (Henry)
2 Nov., Rev. J. W. Ellis

PWH
11 Nov. 1847

Taney County
McCOY, Capt. John

JONES, Elizabeth
14th

SPAD
23 Aug. 1845

Washington County
JOHNSON, B. F.
of Caledonia, MO

COLE, Catherine (ygst., William)
of Bellevue, Washington Co.
21st, Rev. John F. Cowan

HORL
30 Oct. 1845

. . . . . .

Some information -- newspaper, precise date, etc. -- was lost in assembling
these records. The newspapers as shown are believed to be correct. Complete
information can probably be obtained from the clues given -- name of minister,
location, etc. These marriages have not been recorded so far as we can
determine.

ALLEN, Nathan B.
both of this city

ROBAR, Adeline
7 May, Rev. Heim
at Stringtown

SWERE?
14 May 1849

BRACKETT, Wm., Esq.
of Rock Island

SARGENT, Elizabeth M.
of Galena, at St. Louis
21 Oct., Rev. Hawks

SWERE?
29 Oct. 1849

BRADY, Thos.

JONES, Harriet (John Rice)
19

MOG
19 Nov. 1814?

DINWIDDIE, Dr. Archibald
of Howard Co.

HARRIS, Sallie
of Boone Co.
24th ult., Rev. T. C. Harris
(Recorded Boone Co.?)

GLWT
7 April 1853

FARRAR, Benjamin O.	KENNETT, Anne Caroline (L.M.) 24 Dec., Bishop Hawks	SWERE? 31 Dec. 1849
FULTON, Capt. Wm. H. all of Steubenville, Ohio	POWELL, Lavinia C. 25 June, Professor Post, DD	(St. Louis paper) 3 July 1848
GREEN, Dr. Willis M.	FALCONER, Lucy Ann at Chariton n.d., Rev. Fristo	MORE? 27 Sept. 1827
MURRAY, Joseph B. all of this city	GOODEAR, Mrs. Catharine A. 1 Nov., Justice Hale	(St. Louis paper) 5 Nov. 1849
PENDLETON, D. F. of New Orleans	FISHER, Susan A. (eld. Wm. P.) of St. Louis 27 May, Rev. Mr. Capers	(St. Louis paper) 5 June 1848
SMITH, Capt. Isaac of St. Louis	FITHIAN, Elizabeth (Wm. R.) late of Philadelphia, at Cin- cinnati, 18th inst., Rev. Sefton	MORE __? 1846
STOCKTON, Lt. T.B.W.	SMITH, Maria at Prairie du Chien, IL 3rd inst.	MORE 30 March, __?
STOLSON, William	CONN, Eliza 11 May, Justice McKinney	SWERE? 14 May 1849
WALKER, Hiram G.	AMOS, Nancy (Rev. Benj.) at Cole Co., 6 June Rev. Lewis Shelton	MORE ?
WILSON, Wm. E. of New Orleans	MUDGE, Ellen C. (Col. S.H.) at Oakdale, IL 24 May, Rev. Lippinscott	SWERE? 29 May 1848
YOUNG, John	DOIG, Elizabeth (ygst. James) at Dundee,Scotland 10 July, Rev. Islay Burns	SWERE? 13 Aug. 1849